HOW THE LEFT CAN WIN ARGUMENTS
AND INFLUENCE PEOPLE

*Negrophobia and Reasonable Racism: The Hidden Costs of
Being Black in America*
Jody David Armour

Black and Brown in America: The Case for Cooperation
Bill Piatt

Black Rage Confronts the Law
Paul Harris

Selling Words: Free Speech in a Commercial Culture
R. George Wright

*The Color of Crime: Racial Hoaxes, White Fear, Black Protectionism,
Police Harassment, and Other Macroaggressions*
Katheryn K. Russell

The Smart Culture: Society, Intelligence, and Law
Robert L. Hayman Jr.

Was Blind, But Now I See: White Race Consciousness and the Law
Barbara J. Flagg

The Gender Line: Men, Women, and the Law
Nancy Levit

*Heretics in the Temple: Americans Who Reject the Nation's
Legal Faith*
David Ray Papke

*The Empire Strikes Back: Outsiders and the Struggle over
Legal Education*
Arthur Austin

*Interracial Justice: Conflict and Reconciliation in
Post–Civil Rights America*
Eric K. Yamamoto

Black Men on Race, Gender, and Sexuality: A Critical Reader
Edited by Devon Carbado

*When Sorry Isn't Enough: The Controversy over Apologies and
Reparations for Human Injustice*
Edited by Roy L. Brooks

NEW YORK UNIVERSITY PRESS
New York and London

Library of Congress Cataloging-in-Publication Data
Wilson, John K., 1969–
How the left can win arguments and influence people : a tactical
manual for pragmatic progressives / John K. Wilson.
p.   cm.
ISBN 0-8147-9362-2 (cloth) — ISBN 0-8147-9363-0 (pbk.)
1. Liberalism—United States. 2. Progressivism (United States
politics) 3. Right and left (Political science)   I. Title.
JC574.2U6 W57 2001
320.51'3'0973—dc21   2001000739

New York University Press books are printed on acid-free paper,
and their binding materials are chosen for strength and durability.

Manufactured in the United States of America
10 9 8 7 6 5 4 3 2 1

HOW THE LEFT CAN WIN ARGUMENTS AND INFLUENCE PEOPLE

A Tactical Manual for Pragmatic Progressives

John K. Wilson

NEW YORK UNIVERSITY PRESS

New York and London

CONTENTS

Contents

ACKNOWLEDGMENTS

Many people assisted me in writing this book. Niko Pfund, the former editor in chief of New York University Press, along with Richard Delgado and Jean Stefancic, editors of the Critical America series, first approached me with the idea. The book, however, has changed substantially from the original concept.

I thank Stephen Magro, Richard Delgado, Leticia Cortez, and Tom Wilson for reading drafts and making comments. The staff at New York University Press, including Despina Papazoglou Gimbel and Andrew Katz, ably prepared the manuscript for publication. I also owe a debt to too many people and organizations to mention, for their passionate work writing and researching and protesting about the numerous topics discussed in this book.

I encourage readers to praise, vilify, or correct me by e-mail at johnkwilson@postmark.net. Although all mistakes are my own, I will nevertheless deny any errors and then blame them on my political enemies.

THE PROGRESSIVE MAJORITY

How the Left Got Left Behind

This book can be summed up in three words: <u>America is progressive.</u> Unfortunately, many more words are needed to explain why so many people—including so many on the left—believe otherwise.

No, the American public is not likely to go en masse to pick up their Little Red Books of Mao's wisdom, burn American flags, and chant "down with capitalist pigs" on every street corner. Americans are not going to replace the "Star-Spangled Banner" with the "Internationale," bow down before pictures of Stalin, or make a pledge of allegiance to the Communist Manifesto.

This caricature of the "loony left" is one reason that progressives have a level of public respect somewhere between that of lawyers and child molesters. That is, the public vision of a progressive is a tree-hugging, granola-munching professional protester who continuously chants "hey, hey, ho, ho."

The thesis of this book is that a majority of Americans now believe (or could easily be persuaded to believe) in many progressive ideas, even though the power of the progressive movement itself in mainstream politics has largely disintegrated.

In reality, progressives are nearly everywhere, with the possible exception of corporate boardrooms, the White House, and Bob Jones University. Progressives look like everyone else, although they appear to be a little more forlorn than most.

Unfortunately, the progressive views of the American majority do not translate into political power. Progressives cannot sit back and await the rising masses to thrust the left into power. Rather, progressives need to give their potential supporters a reason to be politically active and intellectually interested in the ideas of the left.

If you relied on just the mass media in America or on election results, you would have to conclude that this is a conservative nation. We hear about polls declaring that the American people demand lower taxes, smaller government, the elimination of welfare, the mass execution of criminals, and daily pledges of allegiance to the free market. We see Republicans in charge of Congress, successfully pursuing their goals of putting a prison on every corner and lowering taxes on the wealthy in order to allow economic prosperity to trickle down to everyone else.

America must be conservative. It seems logical, doesn't it? If the Republicans hold political power and the "liberal" Democrats are following their lead, this must mean that the majority of Americans share the values of the right. If the "liberal" media agree with this assessment, then it's surely an established fact: progressivism as a mass movement is dead in America.

Progressivism as an ideology is a powerful force in the American psyche. From environmentalism to feminism to racial equality, Americans believe deeply in progressive ideas. All these ideologies were minority movements just a generation ago; now, however, open opposition to them is considered political suicide in most of the country.

Why, then, does a progressive political movement seem so unthinkable? In a political system controlled by the principle of "one dollar, one vote," these progressive views lose out to the more economically powerful ideas held by the conservative status quo. These progressive ideas end up being ignored by megamedia corporations controlled by the same wealthy forces.

This book is not an attempt to establish a philosophy of the left. Like any political movement, the left has many different philosophies driving its members. Leftists are concerned about civil rights, gay rights, women's rights, poverty, homelessness, education, imprisonment, empowerment, and much more. Leftists believe in liberalism, Marxism, libertarianism, Christianity, and a wide range of other ideologies. Trying to find a common intellectual ground for everything is impossible, since not every leftist can possibly share the same belief in every issue and in what the top priorities should be. Even trying to define what a leftist is seems to be a difficult task, especially since most of the people who believe in leftist ideas may be unwilling to accept the label.

This book is, instead, a guide for political rhetoric and strategic action, a sometimes helpful, sometimes annoying attempt to help the left overcome its own flaws and seek out ways to reach and convince a larger audience about progressive ideas. This is a self-help book for leftists looking for ways to convince the world that what they believe is correct. This book is also a road map showing how the left can turn the public debate to issues they can win.

This book originates from a puzzling paradox: over the past several decades, American political attitudes have become dramatically more progressive. Movements for civil rights, women's equality, and environmental protection, once promoted by a radical fringe, are now fully embraced by the mainstream. Institutions such as Social Security and Medicare, once denounced as socialism, are now the only parts of the government budget regarded as sacrosanct.

At the same time, the political influence of progressives in Washington and around the country has virtually disappeared. Both the Republican Party and the Democrat Party have shifted sharply to the right during the past quarter century even while progressive ideas were becoming more popular.

Never before has the gap between what Americans believe and what the government does been so enormous. Never before have the media been so distant from their audience. Never before have progressives faced this odd situation of winning most of the battles and yet losing the war.

I was born in 1969, perhaps a high point of the left's political influence in America. It was a time when the Great Society and a booming economy coexisted peacefully. Progressives were changing public opinion about the war in Vietnam despite the loss of two leftist martyrs, Robert Kennedy and Martin Luther King Jr. Progressives faced a harsh opposition, but at least there was a sense of growing political influence.

Within a few years, the national scandal of illegal abortions was eliminated (by both court order and growing public opposition), the Vietnam War was halted, the feminist revolution was sweeping the country demanding equality, and the civil rights movement was abolishing openly racist laws.

The change in the American political landscape during the past thirty years has been dramatic. Consider this fact: Richard Nixon was further to the left on most social and economic issues than Bill Clinton. If you don't believe this, look at what happened to the generous welfare programs, high minimum wage, heavy regulation of the economy (such as price controls), lower defense spending (even during the Vietnam War), and small prison population of the early 1970s. This is not an apologia for Nixon, whose crimes were numerous and who undoubtedly would have been even worse than Clinton in our current political environment. But it does show how much politics have changed.

So why did this change occur? Conservatives like to imagine that the change reflects a transformation of what Americans believe. But this transformation was really one of political techniques: our politics has been corporatized. The informal, good ol' boy network has been replaced by political operatives and hired consultants who use all the scientific techniques of polls, voter manipulation, fund-raising, and public relations to bring victory to their clients. Politicians are no longer people with ideas but products to be marketed to a television audience. With the corporatization of politics has come a vast increase in the costs of campaigning and the opportunity for a wealthy conservative elite to increase their control over American elections.

The trend toward progressive attitudes among Americans has only accelerated. Today, Americans advocate gender equality on a level unthinkable at the time I was born, an era when airline stewardess were fired when they turned thirty, got married, or gained fifteen pounds. Today, racial equality is an ideal widely accepted, even if the reality falls short. Today, equality for gays and lesbians is a politically viable possibility, a remarkable leap for an issue that was virtually invisible at the time of the Stonewall riot. Today, environmental awareness and the enormous number of people who recycle would have been unimaginable to the small group of activists who gathered to celebrate the first Earth Day.

Even though the American people have been moving to the left on a number of important issues, the two major political parties have shifted to the right. The left's revival requires both the recognition of the disadvantages it faces and a willingness to fight against those barriers while making use of the advantages that progressives have over the right.

The biggest advantage that the left holds is that it doesn't have to be afraid of speaking the truth to the public. Conservatives, despite their assertions of public support, must always be wary of dealing too openly with Americans. That is, every idea on the right must be carefully vetted to ensure the proper spin control. Even "radical" ideas such as Steve Forbes's flat tax must conceal the extent of tax cuts for the rich under the disguise of a universal tax reduction.

This book argues that progressives need to reshape their arguments and their policy proposals to increase their influence over American politics. It also contends that the left need not sell its soul or jettison its diverse constituents in order to succeed. Rather than moderation, I urge a new kind of tactical radicalism. Rather than a monolithic left focused on class or labor or postmodernism or whatever the pet ideological project of the day is, I advocate a big-tent left capable of mobilizing all its people.

Progressives already have the hearts and minds of the American people. What the left lacks is a political movement to translate that popularity into political action. What the left needs is a rhetorical framework and political plan of action to turn the progressive potential in America into a political force.

Chapter 1

THE DEATH OF SOCIALISM

Dear Comrades:

Socialism is dead. Kaput. Stick a fork in Lenin's corpse. Take the Fidel posters off the wall. Welcome to the twenty-first century. Wake up and smell the capitalism.

I have no particular hostility to socialism. But nothing can kill a good idea in America so quickly as sticking the "socialist" label on it. The reality in America is that socialism is about as successful as Marxist footwear (and have you ever seen a sickle and hammer on anybody's shoes?). Allow your position to be defined as socialist even if it isn't (remember Clinton's capitalist health care plan?), and the idea is doomed.

Instead of fighting to repair the tattered remnants of socialism as a marketing slogan, the left needs to address the core issues of social justice. You can form the word *socialist* from the letters in *social justice*, but it sounds better if you don't. At least 90 percent of America opposes socialism, and 90 percent of America thinks "social justice" might be a good idea. Why alienate so many people with a word?

Even the true believers hawking copies of the *Revolutionary Socialist Worker* must realize by now that the word *socialist* doesn't have a lot of drawing power. In the movie *Bulworth*, Warren Beatty declares: "Let me hear that dirty word: socialism!" *Socialism* isn't really a dirty word, however; if it were, socialism might have a little underground appeal as a forbidden topic. Instead, *socialism* is a forgotten word, part of an archaic vocabulary and a dead language that is no longer spoken in America. Even Michael Harrington, the founder of the Democratic Socialists of America (DSA), didn't use the word *socialism* in his influential book on poverty, *The Other America*.

LABELS FOR LEFTISTS

Labels matter. When we choose to call ourselves *liberal, leftist, neoliberal, Marxist, socialist, Communist, progressive,* or *Democrat*—or have these labels thrust upon us—it affects how people perceive our ideas. Trying to argue with someone while you're wearing a "HELLO, I'm a Marxist" name tag is next to impossible. That doesn't mean labels can be abandoned (it's often not possible), but it does mean that progressives should be aware of their labels' impact.

Leftists don't have a lot of appealing labels, though. A word such as *liberal* is now used as an insult by both the left and the right. To conservatives, any idea conceived in the twentieth century is damned as "liberal," which translates roughly as "spawn of Satan." To leftists, though, "liberal" has become synonymous with the "ineffectual bootlickers in the Democratic Party who kowtow to their corporate masters." Bill Clinton embodies this negative view of liberalism, whether it's from the left and the right, although the two sides violently disagree about what he represents.

That's why "progressive" is probably the best option for leftists looking for a political label. It had a fine tradition in The Progressive Reformists earlier in this century, an excellent leftist magazine of that name and surprisingly little ideological baggage. The right has been so consumed with demonizing the word *liberal* that *progressive* has slipped under their mudslinging radar. Unlike *leftist* or *radical, progressive* doesn't have an extremist tone—after all, who can be opposed to progress? At the same time, it has enough political meaning to prevent most centrists or conservatives from taking it over.

But even if you have a label like *progressive* to describe yourself, the work of political persuasion has barely begun. Because *progressive* is not widely understood in practical terms, leftists need to communicate what progressive ideas look like. Labels and sound bites can't win an argument, but avoiding the unnecessary confusion caused by demonized labels can give progressives an opportunity to make their arguments without being overloaded by negative associations.

The best reason for the left to abandon socialism is not PR but honesty. Most of the self-described "socialists" remaining in America don't qualify as real socialists in any technical sense. If you look at the DSA (whose prominent members include Harvard professor Cornel West and former *Time* columnist Barbara Ehrenreich), most of the policies they urge—a living wage, universal health care, environmental protection, reduced spending on the Pentagon, and an end to corporate welfare—have nothing to do with socialism in the specific sense of government ownership of the means of production. Rather, the DSA program is really nothing more than what a liberal political party ought to push for, if we had one in America.

Europeans, to whom the hysteria over socialism must seem
rather strange, would never consider abandoning socialism as a
legitimate political ideology. But in America, socialism simply
isn't taken seriously by the mainstream. Therefore, if socialists
want to be taken seriously, they need to pursue socialist goals
using nonsocialist rhetoric.

Whenever someone tries to attack an idea as "socialist" (or,
better yet, "communist"), there's an easy answer: Some people
think everything done by a government, from Social Security to
Medicare to public schools to public libraries, is socialism. The
rest of us just think it's a good idea. (Whenever possible, throw
public libraries into an argument, whether it's about good government programs or NEA funding. Nobody with any sense is
opposed to public libraries. They are by far the most popular
government institutions.) If an argument turns into a debate
over socialism, simply define socialism as the total government
ownership of all factories and natural resources—which, since
we don't have it and no one is really arguing for this to happen,
makes socialism a rather pointless debate.

Of course, socialists will always argue among themselves
about socialism and continue their internal debates. But when it
comes to influencing public policy, abstract discussions about socialism are worse than useless, for they alienate the progressive
potential of the American people. It's only by pursuing specific
progressive policies on nonsocialist terms that socialists have
any hope in the long term of convincing the public that socialism isn't (or shouldn't be) a long-dead ideology.

The Fall of the Wall

Of all the events in the twentieth century, perhaps none did
more to aid the progressive cause than the fall of the Berlin Wall
and the collapse of the Soviet Union.

A statement like this may be unfathomable to conservatives who imagine that the death of the Soviet Union was the final nail in the coffin of leftist ideology.

The left did not collapse, however, with the fall of the Berlin Wall for the simple reason that the Soviet Union was never a leftist government. It was, in the words of Ronald Reagan, an "evil empire"—all the more evil from the perspective of progressives because it justified a totalitarian state with pseudoleftist ideology. In recent decades, it has been virtually impossible to find any American leftists beyond a few crackpots, who endorsed the Soviet Union or considered it a genuinely progressive state.

Far from portending the death of the left, the fall of the Soviet Union should be celebrated by progressives for finally permitting a left-wing politics that isn't haunted by the specter of totalitarian communism. Freed from any lingering delusions about a "workers' paradise" in Russia or Poland or Cuba, progressives can now turn their attention to fundamentally reforming domestic policies and addressing globalization.

Progressive Capitalism

The left never has had a kind word for capitalism, which is one reason that progressives are so often marginalized in America, the country where capitalism is the true national religion. From our public celebration of filthy rich business leaders as celebrities to the vast array of magazines and books devoted to revealing the secrets of making money, capitalism is taken for granted.

The left is always taking a dismal view of the American economy, pointing out (accurately) the flaws of our unequal system and its enormous gap between rich and poor. As a result, the "free market" capitalists take credit for the country's tremendous economic success, even though progressive reforms have been largely responsible for the economic growth of the post–World War II era. Because the left refuses to embrace the term (and the right refuses to admit that it exists), the achievements of progressive capitalism have been overlooked.

Although the left regularly criticizes the "free market" capitalist system, the alternatives are rarely discussed. Unfortunately, the left has devoted little attention to what capitalism might look like through progressive eyes. As a result, most people assume that the combination of the "free market" and corporate welfare in America is the only possible form of capitalism.

The right is trying to make itself more appealing by using seemingly contradictory slogans such as George W. Bush's "compassionate conservatism." Similarly, the left needs to challenge the stereotypes of progressives and adopt "capitalism for everyone" as its slogan.

The idea of economic self-determination, a living wage, and equal schools is appealing. The "capitalism for everyone" slogan also has another meaning: instead of capitalism for the big corporation, the rules need to be changed to make sure that capitalism doesn't come at the expense of our environment or the health and safety of our workers.

Progressive capitalism is not a contradiction in terms, for progressives support capitalism in many ways. Even nonprofit organizations and cooperatives are not antithetical to capitalism and the market; these groups simply use capitalism for aims different from the single-minded pursuit of profits. But the rules of supply and demand, the expenses and revenues, the idea of entrepreneurship and innovation, and the need to adapt to the market are essential. Any progressive magazine or institution that tries to defy the rules of capitalism won't be around for very long and certainly won't have the resources to mount a serious advocacy of progressive ideas.

One of the most effective tactics of the environmental movement was encouraging consumers to consider environmental values when making capitalist choices about what products to buy. Today, a manufacturer who ignores environmental issues puts its profits at risk because so many people are looking for environmentally friendly products and packaging. Crusades against Coca-Cola for its massive output of non-recycled plastic bottles in America or against companies supporting foreign dictatorships are part of the continuing battle to force companies to pay attention to consumer demands.

Of course, consumer protests and boycotts are only one part of making "capitalism for everyone." Many progressive groups are now buying stock in companies precisely to raise these issues at stockholder meetings and pressure the companies to adopt environmentally and socially responsible policies.

Unfortunately, the legal system is structured against progressive ideas. In 2000, Ben and Jerry's Ice Cream was forced to sell out to a big corporation that might ignore its commitment to many progressive causes. The company didn't want to sell, but the law demanded that the company's duty to stockholders was to consider only the money involved. Imagine what would happen if our capitalist laws were designed to promote progressive ideas instead of impeding them. Instead of allowing a shareholder lawsuit against any company acting in a morally, socially, and environmentally conscious way, American laws should encourage these goals.

The claim by some leftists that capitalism is inherently irresponsible or evil doesn't make sense. Capitalism is simply a system of markets. What makes capitalism so destructive isn't the basic foundation but the institutions that have been created in the worship of the "free market."

Unfortunately, progressives spend most of their time attacking capitalism rather than taking credit for all the reforms that led to America's economic growth. If Americans were convinced that social programs and investment in people (rather than corporate welfare and investment in weaponry) helped create the current economic growth, they would be far more willing to pursue additional progressive policies. Instead, the left allows conservatives to dismiss these social investments as "too costly" or "big government."

It is crucial not to allow the right to define these progressive programs as "anticapitalist" and then attempt to destroy them. The Reagan/Gingrich/Clinton era's attempt to "get the government off our back" was an effort (fortunately, largely a failure) to corrupt the highly successful progressive capitalism in America. While the Reagan/Gingrich/Clinton "reforms" subsidized the dramatic growth in the wealth of the richest Americans and had a devastating impact on the very poor, they didn't change the basic institutions of progressive capitalism. It may take several generations to recover from the damage done to the poor, but even the far right has been unable (so far) to destroy progressive middle-class institutions such as Social Security or public schools.

Leftists also need to abandon their tendency to make apocalyptic predictions. It's always tempting to predict that environmental destruction is imminent or the stock market is ready to crash in the coming second Great Depression. Arguments that the U.S. economy is in terrible shape fly in the face of reality. It's hard to claim that a middle-class American family with two cars, a big-screen TV, and a computer is oppressed. While the poor in America fell behind during the Reagan/Gingrich/Clinton era and the middle class did not receive its share of the wealth produced during this time, the economy itself is in excellent shape. Instead, the problem is the redistribution of wealth to the very rich under the resurgence of "free market" capitalism.

Instead of warning that the economy will collapse without progressive policies, the left should emphasize that the progressive aspects of American capitalism have created the current success of the American economy after decades of heavy government investment in human capital. But the cutbacks in investment for education and the growing disparity between the haves and the have-nots are threatening the economy's future success.

Capitalism for Everyone

Capitalism is far too ingrained in American life to eliminate. If you go into the most impoverished areas of America, you will find that the people who live there are not seeking government control over factories or even more social welfare programs; they're hoping, usually in vain, for a fair chance to share in the capitalist wealth. The poor do not pray for socialism—they strive to be a part of the capitalist system. They want jobs, they want to start businesses, and they want to make money and be successful.

What's wrong with America is not capitalism as a system but capitalism as a religion. We worship the accumulation of wealth and treat the horrible inequality between rich and poor as if it were an act of God. Worst of all, we allow the government to exacerbate the financial divide by favoring the wealthy: go anywhere in America, and compare a rich suburb with a poor town—the city services, schools, parks, and practically everything else will be better financed in the place populated by rich people.

The aim is not to overthrow capitalism but to overhaul it. Give it a social-justice tune-up, make it more efficient, get the economic engine to hit on all cylinders for everybody, and stop putting out so many environmentally hazardous substances.

To some people, this goal means selling out leftist ideals for the sake of capitalism. But the right thrives on having an ineffective opposition. The Revolutionary Communist Party helps stabilize the "free market" capitalist system by making it seem as if the only alternative to free-market capitalism is a return to Stalinism. Prospective activists for change are instead channeled into pointless discussions about the revolutionary potential of the proletariat. Instead of working to persuade people to accept progressive ideas, the far left talks to itself (which may be a blessing, given the way it communicates) and tries to sell copies of the *Socialist Worker* to an uninterested public.

yes, big problem

A lot of progressives out there are doing a lot of good, of course: they're defending the poor in court, providing social services, educating the children, helping the homeless, and protecting the environment. The one thing they're usually not doing, however, is reaching out to the mass public with effective communication about the ideas underlying these actions.

By simply condemning capitalism, progressives help spread the idea that "free market" capitalism is a natural phenomenon, but that is a myth told by economics professors. Like Santa Claus, the "free market" is imagined to be an all-powerful force of justice that allocates lots of money to the homes of good little boys and girls and leaves only lumps of low-grade coal in the stockings of bad children. If you have no money and no presents, the fault is your own and not Santa's or the market's.

Like Santa Claus, the myth of the "free market" promotes the idea that the current allocation of resources is an inevitable and ideal distribution that cannot be challenged. And like Santa Claus, the "free market" promotes the destructive notion that people who are given gifts (usually their family's wealth) have somehow earned them, whereas the poor get what they deserve.

The "free market" resembles Santa in another way: much of what the wealthy receive is not created by them but is given to them. The children of the wealthy get all the advantages money can buy, plus well-funded top-notch public schools, special preferences to enter private colleges, and all the networking connections that are crucial to business success today. The very rich who make their money in the stock market also pay less in taxes than does a construction worker, and because of tax breaks and regressive Social Security and sales taxes, many rich Americans pay less of their income in taxes than do the working poor. Add to this the corporate welfare at all levels of government, and the Santa Claus aspect of the "free market" economy becomes readily apparent.

Progressives are not demanding a Robin Hood approach, stealing from the rich and giving to the poor; they simply want the rich to pay their fair share to create an egalitarian society that is necessary for future economic development. This isn't a "screw the rich" argument: it's an argument that government should stop screwing the poor. Equal opportunity should really mean equal opportunity, and we shouldn't have a government that gives more benefits to the wealthiest corporations than it provides to the poorest homeless people in our society.

The Rise of American Socialism

Socialists who are nervous about abandoning their philosophy to embrace some wishy-washy progressive version of capitalism shouldn't be worried. American progressives are not destroying socialism; they're taking socialism, kicking and screaming, into the twenty-first century.

What postwar America has represented is not a vast expansion of capitalism but a new, better form of socialism. The new, American-style socialism is a grand experiment in the importance of human capital rather than old-fashioned industrial capital, and it has been much more efficient than previous forms of either capitalism or socialism.

Old-style socialism, with its government-controlled planned economy, failed because it neglected the human element. Old-style capitalism, with its privately controlled (but government-subsidized) economy, also neglected human beings. As technological advances made the agricultural and industrial economies obsolete, old-style socialism and old-style capitalism were discarded on the junk heap of history.

The problem is that while everybody recognizes the failure of old-style socialism, the failure of old-style capitalism goes largely unnoticed. That's because Americans have a curious blind spot when it comes to the socialist aspects of their society. Socialism as a political movement has been so thoroughly crushed by the mainstream political parties that any admission of socialist change is unthinkable. Instead, Americans hold dearly to the myth that the success of the United States is due to its "free market" capitalism.

Leftists are too often guilty of accepting the right's propaganda that a particular version of capitalism is its inevitable form. "Free market" capitalism is not the natural state of capitalism because capitalism doesn't have a natural state. All forms of capitalism work within a set of government regulations and social institutions without which it could not exist. The "free" market has never existed and would quickly be stopped by popular acclaim if it ever did come into being.

The "triumph" of American capitalism in the twentieth century has far more to do with the limits imposed on "free" markets than the mechanical operation of supply and demand. Free public education, government-sponsored research, antitrust regulations, the progressive income tax, environmental improvements, the social welfare system, subsidized medical care, antidiscrimination laws—all these efforts were crucial to the success of American capitalism. Without all these progressive institutions, America—despite its enormous natural resources—

might not have become the world's economic superpower, and it certainly would not have achieved its current levels of wealth.

Most of American history is a testament to the outright failure of "free market" capitalism. Old-style capitalism, embodied by the robber barons and the horrors of the early industrial economy in America, failed miserably. Compared with the era of progressive capitalism in the past fifty years, the earlier periods of "free market" capitalism brought us dire poverty and slow economic growth. Most of that growth was due to the "free" land stolen from Native Americans and huge natural resources such as oil and coal found on that land, as well as the geographic isolation that protected America from destructive European conflicts. Contrary to the assertions of "free market" advocates, it was the gradual introduction of progressive reforms during the twentieth century that created most of the successful economic growth that is mistakenly attributed to "free market" capitalism.

The economic growth, technological improvements, and medical and scientific advances of the postwar era (1945–2000) exceed by a wide margin all the accomplishments made by "free market" capitalism in earlier centuries. The reason for this economic advancement in America was that the United States, more than any other nation, adopted a program of forward-looking "socialism of human capital."

Socialism is all about the equitable distribution of the means of production. Under old-style socialism, this meant government control of industrial plants. But in a new economic age in which human capital overwhelms industrial capital, socialism must adapt. Today's socialism of human capital means equalizing the opportunities for education, health, and job opportunities.

Whereas "free market" capitalism is a failed, conservative economic philosophy that entrenches the inefficient prejudices of the day, new-style socialism has fought to bring all people into the capitalist system. The inclusion of women and minorities in the workplace at productive jobs—a reform forced by progressives—has done more to improve capitalist productivity in American than any idea pushed by the advocates of "free-market" capitalism. This American socialism has enabled the capitalist economy to succeed to a degree that the disciples of capitalism could never imagine. It's little wonder that so many conventional economists are befuddled by the idea of a growing economy with higher wages and lower unemployment.

The Social Security and labor rights established in the 1930s, the GI Bill in the 1940s, the educational improvements of the 1950s, the antipoverty programs and huge investment in higher education of the 1960s, and the antidiscrimination laws of the 1960s and 1970s, the environmental movement—all these investments in human capital gave America a huge advantage over the rest of the world. This is the future of socialism, ironically achieved in its highest form by the country that so decisively rejects socialism.

So why not call it socialism instead of progressivism? There is a very good reason, aside from the tremendous antipathy for the word *socialism*. Most of all, distinguishing the "socialism of human capital" from the old "socialism of industrial capital" is extraordinarily confusing. Most people think that "socialism" means nationalizing industries. The fact that the new socialism accomplishes the goal of human equality far better than the old socialism should be enough to recommend it.

Another reason to abandon the term *socialism* is that the socialism of human capital is roughly the same as the capitalism of human capital. When the focus is on human investment, the old debate between socialism and capitalism is outmoded. The new socialism does not destroy capitalism: it beats capitalism at its own game.

The goal of the "socialism of human capital" is to increase the investment in people and to equalize this investment. This progressive movement has done far more to save American capitalism than the capitalists themselves ever did: it educated their employees, provided them with a subsidized pension plan and welfare system, increased the labor supply by enforcing equality, and cleaned up the mess the corporations made.

Conservatives have frequently attacked the progressive advances in America, from Social Security to Medicare, as a form of socialism. And they're right. This is socialism in the new sense. Building on the progressive successes of the past century and expanding the social investment of this new socialism are the goals of today's progressives. Abandoning the old socialism, including its outmoded rhetoric, is the key to creating the ideals which socialists are seeking.

Chapter 2

THE VAST RIGHT-WING CONSPIRACY (AND WHY THE LEFT-WING NEEDS ONE, TOO)

Hillary Clinton is famous for describing a "vast right-wing conspiracy" against her husband. She was both right and wrong. There was a massive, quasi-organized scheme (call it a conspiracy if you like) by the far right to dig up all the dirt on Bill Clinton.

But Hillary was wrong to think it was bad for the country: The vast right-wing conspiracy prompted a lot of soul-searching about Clinton, and we found out he didn't have one. The conspiracy dug up some of the ugly truth about Clinton's propensity to lie, cheat, and squirm. (It also prompted a lot of crackpot hallucinations about Clinton as a political mafioso ordering the murder of his enemies and Vince Foster.)

This vast right-wing conspiracy didn't begin with Bill Clinton. For more than two decades, conservatives have been financing a remarkably effective effort to put right-wing ideas into the mainstream media. From think tanks turning out op-eds to subsidized conservative student newspapers, the right has created an intensive propaganda campaign to denounce the possibility of progressive ideas and push conservative solutions to our problems.

Some people are upset at the idea of calling anything a "conspiracy." And of course, far right strategists do not hold secret meetings at which they talk about how they're going to control the country. In an age of alien autopsies, the phrase "conspiracy theory" is a joke. Even so, the well-organized conservative movement, from the religious right to the libertarians to the cultural conservatives, has had an undeniable influence on public policy.

The right-wing conspiracy in itself isn't the real threat to leftists; it's the total absence of a similarly well-organized left-wing conspiracy. That's what keeps progressives so powerless. A left-wing conspiracy to increase progressive voices in the mainstream is an important step in changing the political establishment. Obviously, a leftist conspiracy by itself won't change policies, but it will give progressives a better opportunity to influence the public debate.

The left needs to study the vast right-wing conspiracy not just in order to understand it but also to imitate it. Progressives may never have the money or the media influence of the right-wing conspiracy. One hopes that a left-wing conspiracy would be fairer and more honest than its right-wing counterpart. Progressives have a lot of lessons to learn in order to create a vast left-wing conspiracy.

Conservatives and the Mechanisms of Control

Conservatives in America maintain their political influence with the power of money and a well-organized movement.

The right, as well, has also used carefully chosen rhetoric to win political power, though they haven't yet persuaded Americans to endorse most of their conservative ideas. The right has, however, been able to discredit leftist ideas and keep them out of the mainstream.

Newt Gingrich's political action committee, GOPAC, once sent a pamphlet to Republicans entitled *Language, a Key Mechanism of Control* which offered to help candidates "speak like Newt." The National Conference of Teachers of English even awarded it their annual Doublespeak Award. As a Gingrich spokesman noted, "Obviously, the general concept is something Newt has been pressing in his public speaking for a long time, that Republicans need to use vivid language to describe the values of people we oppose politically."

To this end, Gingrich provided lists of both "positive, governing words" and "negative, name-calling words."

NEWT'S POSITIVE, GOVERNING WORDS

Active(ly)	Control
Activist	Courage
Building	Crusade
Candid(ly)	Debate
Care(ing)	Dream
Challenge	Duty
Change	Eliminate good-time in prison
Children	Empower(ment)
Choice/choose	Fair
Citizen	Family
Commitment	Freedom
Common sense	Hard work
Compete	Help
Confident	Humane
Conflict	Incentive

Initiative

Lead

Learn

Legacy

Liberty

Light

Listen

Mobilize

Moral

Movement

Opportunity

Passionate

Peace

Pioneer

Precious

Premise

Preserve

Principle(d)

Pristine

Pro-(issue) flag, children,
   environment

Prosperity

Protect

Proud/pride

Provide

Reform

Rights

Share

Strength

Success

Tough

Truth

Unique

Vision

We/us/our

Workfare

Newt's Name-Calling Words

Anti-(issue) flag, family, child,
   jobs

Betray

Coercion

Collapse

Consequences

Corruption

Crisis

Decay

Deeper

Destroy

Destructive

Devour

Endanger

Failure

Greed

Hypocrisy

Ideological

Impose

Incompetent

Insecure

Liberal

Lie

Limit(s)

Pathetic

Permissive attitude

Radical

Self-serving

Sensationalists	Traitors
Shallow	Unionized bureaucracy
Sick	Urgent
They/them	Waste
Threaten	

Some of Gingrich's "words" are just bizarre ("eliminate good-time in prison" is one of the "positive, governing" words), while others reveal how far the politics of denunciation has come. When Newt Gingrich is urging Republicans to attack their opponents as "pathetic," "sick," "incompetent" "traitors" who want to "destroy," "devour," and "betray" Americans, it shows that going negative can be a powerful tactic.

Two important words are missing from Gingrich's "positive" list: equality and justice. The fact that Gingrich leaves them out of such an all-encompassing list is significant. It can't be because the words are unpopular: from the Fourteenth Amendment to the pledge of allegiance, these words (along with *liberty*) are among a handful of sacred concepts in American history. How, then, could Gingrich omit them? The reason must have been this: equality and justice can only rarely be invoked to describe Republican policies.

Equality and justice are dangerous concepts to the right wing, powerful ideas that are difficult to keep under their careful "mechanism of control." It must have seemed better to Gingrich to put equality and justice under wraps than to risk allowing such ideas to become the focal point of any debate. Unlike Gingrich's other simplistic sound bites, equality and justice have a deep meaning etched in history that can be invoked by anyone. A Republican candidate who urges a policy based on the principle of equality could quickly be asked why we have so much inequality in America. A demand for justice on some issue could lead to a request for a just society. Thus it is better, Republicans seem to think, to let dangerous ideas like these be ignored and forgotten.

For progressives, focusing on these broad positive concepts—and developing specific policies to advance equality and justice—is the key to a successful argument.

The primary mechanism of control that Gingrich gave his fellow Republicans to exercise is not merely control over positive and negative phrases. Rather, the larger goal is controlling what is not spoken. By keeping the debate within a narrow battleground of a handful of words, Gingrich was able to avoid the danger of allowing words such as *justice* and *equality* to enter a discussion at all. Republicans aren't supposed to argue about deep ideas, according to Gingrich's pamphlet; they should simply ignore them and move on to the next insult on the list and the next "positive, governing" word about their own policies. Gingrich's goal was not simply to control the language used by Republicans but to control all the language used in debates, to put everything on their turf and on their terms.

Progressives do not need a set of simplistic sound bites (although Gingrich's list, with a few changes, can work for anyone of any ideology who wants to do that) but a way to change the political debate.

Words matter. The use of certain words can sway an opponent to your side. The use of other words can drive a potential sympathizer away. But words are not weapons that can be disconnected from ideas and tossed around effectively. Progressives can win only by getting their ideas discussed, not by joining the sound bite game.

Gingrich's goal for the Republicans was to play the politics of distraction, to toss around words in order to prevent a serious public debate. If ideas and not words become the focus of public discussion, progressives have an opportunity to prevail. That's why they must recognize the Gingrich approach but never imitate it.

Carefully choosing the words you use is not the same as adopting language as a mechanism of control. Selectivity is not manipulation, and using rhetoric that helps people better understand what you're saying is not dishonest.

On the negative side, it's worth noting that both *liberal* and *radical* make the list of right-wing insults, whereas a more positive word like *progressive* is nowhere to be found. *Communist* and *socialist* are so completely out of favor that Gingrich doesn't even bother listing them, perhaps because a genuinely socialist opponent is so rarely encountered that trying to pin the label on him would be more of a joke than an advantage. *Unionized bureaucracy* is also on Gingrich's debit list—again, it's important to realize that although demonizing union workers is considered a dangerous game, union leaders and "the bureaucracy" are always open to attack.

Because Gingrich was afraid of attacking basic progressive principles, owing to their popularity, he was forced to smear opponents with hate words rather than engage their arguments. But because the media rarely go beyond the sound bites and almost never allow a progressive voice to refute them, Gingrich's framework was politically successful.

Gingrich and the Republicans imagined that elections were won and lost in the rhetorical battlefield and that the proper phrase could determine the fate of a candidate. No magic words can win arguments. Using popular terms in place of unpopular ones can lure a few votes, but it cannot change the terms of an election. Words without meaning are empty and powerless, and they are what have infected far too many American political debates.

People are not rhetorical robots responding to certain words with a programmed, uncontrolled reaction. Rather, people react to ideas in a context shaped by the words they use. Changing the rhetoric of the left thus requires as much transformation in the places where these arguments take place as it does in the words used to promote progressive ideas.

The dilemma for progressives is trying to use language as effectively as the right and center have, but without the same level of dishonesty. Progressives usually have the advantage of being correct, but the truth doesn't always win an argument.

At some point, the left must also overcome its deep suspicion of democracy. After years of being told by the corporate media that the public doesn't want to hear progressive ideas, after years of being told by corporate publishers that there isn't a market for the left, progressives have often believed this rhetoric; maybe, we think, the public really is just stupid and happy to stay that way.

We shouldn't, however, blame people for failing to buy a book no one ever told them about, for failing to consider ideas that the media won't reveal to them. Democracy didn't fail the left; it simply hasn't been tried yet. Progressives should be skeptical of abandoning the public and imagining that they can take power by following in the footsteps of the right, that is, by using money and influence peddling to try to get their way. As many gays who dumped large amounts of money into Democratic coffers learned, progressive policies cannot win in a corrupt system.

It's difficult for progressives to write and speak to a broad audience when it's nearly impossible for most of them to reach anyone other than fellow leftists. Because writers and speakers adapt their message to a particular audience, it was only natural for progressives to seek out a rhetoric comfortable for other progressives, even if it wasn't the most persuasive message to send out to a larger group.

Such rhetoric, however, has made it even harder to progressives to seek out a mainstream audience and create a convincing message for the wider public. Instead, the left has descended into more and more internal bickering about its ideological goals, all the while losing the real war for the hearts and minds of Americans.

GOING NEGATIVE

Newt Gingrich was the poster child for going negative in political debates, with mixed results. Although Gingrich's harsh attacks on Democrats and liberals helped unify Republicans against a common enemy, it was a unity without a common foundation, because Gingrich never established a positive vision for running the country after the Contract with America was defeated.

Going negative is easier than developing a positive vision because more people disagree with a particular idea than agree with any individual alternative to it. Nearly all Americans could agree with Gingrich's assessment of the Democratic Congress as a corrupt institution. The problem was that most Americans (correctly) regarded Gingrich as corrupt after he took power.

Going negative is also a tactic that gets attention. Denouncing the current system will always draw more reporters than will a weak proposal for reform. John McCain's denunciations of the current campaign finance system brought him much more publicity than a purely positive approach would have done. In fact, McCain's refusal to specifically attack his Senate colleagues (or mention his own flaws) prevented even more media attention to this issue.

Progressives should not underestimate the power of negativity. Going negative is always the approach used by a political movement with little power. The progressives need to understand, however, that going negative can never substitute for an effective political movement. Going negative may work for last-minute thirty-second TV commercials in a campaign, but it can't sustain a large crusade to change American politics. A positive agenda is always needed to contrast with the ideas being attacked.

How the Right Won the Culture Wars

The right's victory in the public sphere was not a triumph of logic over emotion or the victory of rational argument over inferior ideas. That's not how our system works. Progressives have failed to realize that winning an argument doesn't mean winning the war. Although more Americans than ever before share progressives ideas and although many of these leftist beliefs (including gender equality, racial equality, environmentalism, and support for many social programs) now dominate the mainstream, the left itself is losing ground as a political force.

The right wing won the culture wars in the same way they have taken control of our political system: with money. It's more complicated than that, of course, it always is. Part of the story includes clever organizing by the far right, the growing corporatization of the media, and the failure of the left to create an effective resistance. But ultimately, money mattered, and the right simply overwhelmed the progressives with its financial investment in an ideological struggle.

One small piece of this battle was in publishing. Virtually every important right-wing book in the 1990s was created and promoted with the help of tens of thousands (in some cases, hundreds of thousands) of dollars in support from right-wing foundations. From Dinesh D'Souza's *Illiberal Education* to Charles Murray's *The Bell Curve*, from the *National Review* to the *American Spectator*, these ideas were subsidized and publicized, played up by op-eds and reviews written at right-wing think tanks, and aggressively promoted in the well-financed right-wing magazines.

D'Souza is a perfect example of how right-wing money helps shape the public debate over the culture wars. D'Souza entered the conservative network in college as editor of the *Dartmouth Review*, which reveled in printing racism, such as an interview with former Ku Klux Klan leader David Duke (illustrated on the cover with a photo of a black man being lynched on campus). The *Review* received a $10,000 grant from a conservative foundation in 1980, and numerous other right-wing papers were given similar funds to promote the campaign against what became known as "political correctness." After writing a fawning biography of Jerry Falwell, D'Souza was able to get a $30,000 grant from the Olin Foundation to write his book *Illiberal Education*, plus a $20,000 grant to promote the book and a $98,400 research fellowship at the American Enterprise Institute in 1991 when the book appeared. Since then, D'Souza has profited handsomely by the playing the role of a second-rate right-wing journalist turned public intellectual with the help of generous conservative money.

This doesn't mean that authors are moving to the right in order to make a buck (although it would be a rational plan for any upwardly mobile intellectual—I'm currently open to any and all offers of bribery to turn against the left). Instead, people who would toil in obscurity on the left are heavily promoted and subsidized because they're right wingers. The right wing gives its people training and encouragement, money and promotion, think tank positions and "research" fellowships. The left, though, offers virtually nothing except the certainty of another leftist's criticism.

The right's money also bought it organizing strength. From the Moral Majority to the Christian Coalition to the Promise Keepers, the religious right can mobilize a large number of people. Newt Gingrich himself was fined by Congress for illicitly funneling money from corporate friends to his personal nonprofit organizations (with the taxpayers paying for the tax deductions) in order to train the Republican activists he hoped would put him in the presidency.

Whining about the vast right-wing conspiracy is a popular

sport among progressives, but it accomplishes remarkably little. Most people simply don't care about the gripes of poor oppressed leftists. Although it may be effective to point out the way that conservative foundations subsidize attack journalism that is depicted as objective scholarship in the mainstream media, progressives ultimately need to make arguments work on their own merits.

Conservatives argue that the conspiracy is really on the left, because large foundations such as Ford and MacArthur have liberal tendencies. Of course, this is true if you imagine that helping the poor is left-wing idea. Although many foundations are liberal leaning, they mostly serve the function of a shadow government, providing basic health, community, culture, and human services that the government offers in most other countries. The liberalism of foundations is a basic respect for all people, not a political ideology geared toward changing media coverage and government policies, as the conservative foundations aim to do.

In their book *No Mercy*, which analyzes how right-wing foundations won the culture wars, Richard Delgado and Jean Stefanic wrote:

> America works best when it receives a roughly equal infusion of ideas from the right and the left. For nearly two decades, this balance has been tilting sharply. Today, society is out of kilter, the right in full cry, the left defeated and listless. Most new programs and initiatives come from the right. The left has had little to do with setting the country's agenda and seems unable to mount any sort of effective resistance to the conservative juggernaut.

To fight the right, progressives must organize an opposition to the current system that challenges the status quo and brings popular progressive ideas into mainstream debates.

Creating the Vast Left-Wing Conspiracy

Creating a progressive conspiracy won't be easy, as it will take organization, money, intelligence, and determination. The left can hold all the conferences it wants, but progressives won't build a conspiracy until they identify their signature issues and make plans for action that go beyond the usual tried and true tactics of the left.

An effective conspiracy doesn't need to be a secret. The vast right-wing conspiracy has been written about and discussed a thousand times, but this hasn't diminished its effectiveness. To the contrary, publicity builds credibility for any respectable conspiracy. Newt Gingrich—one of the key components of the vast right-wing conspiracy in the Republican Party—was quite open about his plans to take over the country. Gingrich's propaganda wing, GOPAC, would send out to anyone (including me) its audio cassettes of speeches advising Republican candidates how to tailor their messages to ensure a Republican-controlled Congress.

Although the conservative conspiracy united behind its hatred of Bill Clinton, the far right had organized effectively long before that to promote their ideas.

A similar public conspiracy of the left is needed that can promote progressive arguments. Unfortunately, progressives are terrible at creating conspiracies. Perhaps it was the red-baiting of McCarthyism and the COINTELPRO of the FBI that undermined effective conspiracies on the left. The closest that progressives come to a vast conspiracy is when they hold a protest. However, protesting isn't always the most effective tactic. For example, research showing the large number of mistakes made in death penalty cases and students investigating how innocent people are held on death row is far more effective than a thousand protests of chanting activists.

This doesn't mean that protests are worthless. As the World Trade Organization (WTO) and International Monetary Fund (IMF) protests in Seattle and Washington and the Million Mom March against guns showed, creative and massive protests can be a powerful way to bring attention to an issue that would otherwise be ignored.

When protests are held too often on issues that are too familiar, the result is "protest fatigue." A protest every week on the outrage of the day soon bores the media, the politicians, the public, and the protesters themselves. The press might cover the protest, but it will include snide comments about the size of the crowd and only indifferent attention to the issue at hand. This doesn't mean that progressives need to abandon protests as a tactic but that protests need to be coordinated with other efforts.

One step in making a vast left-wing conspiracy is manipulating the media. All the leftist think tanks and experts in the world won't matter if the press continues to rely on the conservative and establishment figures for their sound bites.

Writing letters to the editor complaining about media bias and inaccuracy is a long-favored technique of conservatives. It's effective, too: most studies show that the letters column has more readers than the rest of the op-ed pages. Don Wycliff, public editor of the *Chicago Tribune*, noted late in the 2000 campaign that "virtually all the complaints about campaign coverage seem to come from the George W. Bush camp—or his camp followers." The conservatives rants powerfully influence the media by reinforcing the myth of the liberal media. When I complained to the media magazine *Brill's Content* about its choice of Newt Gingrich's pollster Frank Luntz to do a "neutral" poll about the media, Steven Brill responded that he chose Luntz because "we get criticized for being too much on the left." *Brill's Content* is a thoroughly mainstream corporate magazine, but conservatives are able to manipulate its content by force of complaint.

HOW TO GET A LETTER PUBLISHED

Letters to the editor are a powerful way of influencing the media and also getting progressive ideas in the public eye. Most national newspapers such as the *New York Times* and the *Washington Post* are highly selective, but many smaller community newspapers will publish just about anything. Here's a list of what to keep in mind:

Be nice. Never insult or question the credibility of the publication, even if it deserves it. One might hope that journalists had the courage to print scathing criticism of themselves, but don't bet on it. I've written dozens of letters that never saw print because of my excessive enthusiasm for telling the truth.

Keep it short. Remember, editors are lazy. They don't want to edit letters (but they sometimes will). They always prefer a concise letter to a long, rambling diatribe. And it's better to write a short letter than to have your argument cut to pieces because of space limitations. Look at the publication you're writing to in order to get a sense of the normal preferred length for letters.

Respond to the story. A letter is not the opportunity to fulfill your literary talents. Stay close to the piece you're writing about. Some newspapers will publish occasional letters from out of left field, but it's rare. If you feel inspiration on some subject, try submitting a op-ed if the newspaper accepts them, or wait for the right topic to pop up in the paper.

Write it quickly. If you mail a letter one week after a story appears, it will have virtually no chance of getting published in a major newspaper. Use e-mail, and respond within one day. That gives the editor more time to find a space for it, and readers are more likely to remember the original article.

Say something interesting. This is easier said than done, but it's crucial. Mere disagreement or outrage is not grounds for having a letter published. Finding an original position or an original way of phrasing an argument greatly increases the likelihood of having a letter accepted. Don't repeat an argument that's already been made (or attacked) in the op-ed pages—instead, try to surprise the op-ed editor with an idea that hasn't been considered. If you don't have a good idea, don't bother writing.

Do not quote anyone (unless you're repeating something from the original story). This is not the time (is there ever a time?) to haul out the Bartlett's for the perfect quotation from Shakespeare. Nor is it the time to quote Marx, Lenin, Chomsky, or anybody else. The Bible may be quoted against religious conservatives, but that's the only exception.

Use your status. If you are a professor or an expert on the topic, you should mention it in the byline. High-status writers are more likely to get published and to convince readers if their status is listed after their name in the newspaper.

Be aware of syndication. If you want to write something against a syndicated columnist, it's possible to write the same letter to many different newspapers, using the web to find out where the column appeared. Be careful: most newspapers hate this, and if you do it often, you'll end up on a letter-writing blacklist (no one will admit it, but every newspaper has a group of people it usually bars from publication). The major media will check to make sure you wrote the letter and haven't submitted it any-where else.

Document your facts. If you are including facts or statistics (usu-ally you shouldn't) that weren't published by the newspaper, in-clude the references where this information can be checked (as a postscript). Editors don't want to print factual errors in the letter column, and it's easiest for them to throw a letter away if it in-cludes any questionable numbers.

Simply writing a letter to the editor isn't enough: progressives need to call, write, and e-mail the reporters and news editors as well, to voice their concerns and suggest organizations and experts who should be contacted the next time something is written on this topic. And when your letter to the editor concerns state or national legislation, copies should also go to your representatives.

Conservatives in America have become professional whiners, complaining about the repression of their ideas at every turn, with catchphrases about the "liberal media" or "political correctness" to prove their oppression. Progressives also need to learn how to whine, not how to grouse with one's comrades over a cup of java in some anticorporate coffeehouse, but how to whine effectively to the right people in the right way.

Progressives also need to create local and national media watchdog organizations that can apply pressure on the mainstream media. Refusing to allow the center-right media to be defined as "liberal" and pressuring reporters to include progressive ideas will have a ripple effect: politicians will pay attention to what the media are focusing on, and the public will support progressive ideas when they have an opportunity to hear them.

Progressives can't depend on the mainstream media to represent the ideas of the left. Instead, progressives need to create their own print, broadcast, and Internet media. This doesn't mean that the left has to create more magazines for its internal consumption. Although it's important to have political magazines and newspaper aimed at the left, progressives have a more important task in bringing these stories to a wider audience. Finding the talent and content is fairly simple; there are plenty of progressive journalists and commentators around. The problem is the lack of jobs and the absence of alternative media in which progressive journalists are free to pursue stories critical of the status quo.

The left also needs to imitate the right by supporting a national network of progressive student and local newspapers, along with progressive radio, television, and Internet efforts. Local and campus media also are important to train the next generation of progressive thinkers and journalists. The far right created many of the campus newspapers to train future "journalists" and then used their connections with the establishment to place these young thinkers in important jobs. The left must do the same, especially because the number of jobs in progressive media is limited. Progressive student media—whether in the form of broadcasting, print, or Internet—are crucial to training the future progressive media professionals and giving them credentials to enter the mainstream.

Progressives created a loose network of newspapers under the guidance of the underfunded Center for Campus Organizing, but there never were any financial assistance, training conferences, guidance on how to sustain an alternative newspaper, or work to move these individuals into mainstream journalism after graduation. Most of these alternative newspapers live on the fringes, quickly going out of business or barely surviving for lack of support.

When progressive groups want to draw attention to an overlooked issue, they'll often spend thousands of dollars to run an ad in the mainstream newspaper—which has failed to write about the topic. Meanwhile, free alternative progressive newspapers in many urban areas could be sustained with this money and advertising from other progressive groups. But many progressive organizations have a prejudice against advertising (and, to be fair, very little money to buy it) and a deep suspicion of PR campaigns.

Alternative newspapers were once an important source of progressive ideas in an era of growing media consolidation and one-newspaper towns. But now the alternative newspapers are themselves becoming corporatized, getting rid of left-oriented views and investigative journalism in favor of soft, feature-oriented approaches.

The left needs to win back these alternative newspapers and to create inexpensive, high-quality newspapers as alternatives to them. The public still wants to read muckraking journalism; the problem is that the economics of journalism makes newspapers dependent on advertisers and a demographic focused on yuppies. Still, there is an opportunity for genuinely progressive publications to succeed by reaching a mass audience. The problems are that the progressive-minded foundations won't support them (publications are usually specifically excluded from applying for many grants); progressive-minded groups and businesses won't advertise in them; and the result is that leftists are unable to create alternatives to the mainstream corporate press.

The rise of the Internet has given progressives viable alternatives to the mainstream media. E-mail has been critical to the left to organize national movements such as the demonstrations against the WTO in Seattle and to exchange information. Web sites enable progressive organizations to make knowledge widely available at a minimal cost. The Internet cannot completely replace physical newspapers and magazines, however. It is important, but most people still want to read ink on paper.

Even on the Internet, progressives are starting to show the same problems they face in print and broadcast media: despite the openness of the web, corporate America is quickly starting to control cyberspace. There is no starting point for progressives on the web, no search engine for people seeking the truth, and no outreach to bring the masses to sites with progressive information. Many of the progressive web sites are excellent, but few people can find them. The web, like the rest of the world, is increasingly dominated by corporate money.

The notion that the left has no money is a myth that must be challenged. Plenty of leftists have plenty of money, and lots of progressive-minded organizations have lots of resources. The problem is that most of this money isn't always used effectively. For example, it's given to academics and community groups rather than being targeted to public debates. It's spent by unions on wasted donations to the procorporate Democratic Party.

A vast conspiracy works only if it has a wide range of participants. To be successful, a conspiracy needs both idealists contemplating utopian thoughts and pragmatists pushing for a tactical advantage; insiders pursuing progressive approaches in the corridors of power and outsiders waging a relentless attack on the establishment; true believers urging progressives to remain faithful to their principles and skeptics questioning both the goals and the tactics of the left. Above all else, a vast conspiracy is also a vast conversation on the left, a conversation about what can be done to gain political power.

A vast left-wing conspiracy cannot be created in a day; the vast right-wing conspiracy emerged only after decades of dedicated work and funding, with the inspiration of conservative leaders and the strong support of leading right-wing institutions. But there still is hope for the left: if the progressive movement, although politically powerless, nevertheless has values that are broadly supported by the American people, imagine how much change would be possible if the left were a politically vibrant and influential movement in the United States.

Chapter 3

THE FAILURE OF CENTRISM AND THE FALL OF THE DEMOCRATIC PARTY

"We restored the vital center," declared Bill Clinton in his final State of the Union address. But the only center Clinton brought to America was the vitiated center, an empty hole in our political soul filled up with campaign contributions, piles of polls, and broken promises.

Clinton, the leading Democratic advocate for centrism as head of the Democratic Leadership Council (DLC), was fortunate to rule during a period of economic expansion (which he had virtually no part in creating) that made centrism tolerable enough that Clinton won't be known as one of the worst presidents in history. One can only imagine how Clinton's political and sexual errors would be judged if he had had the misfortune to preside during an economic downturn caused by forces largely beyond his control, as Jimmy Carter did.

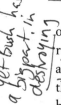

yet Bush has a big part in destroying

Viewed in purely political terms, Clinton's centrism was a failure. Personally, Clinton was able to serve two terms as president. However, under his leadership, the Democratic Party performed miserably. Clinton helped the Democrats lose Congress to the Republicans, and dozens of governors and state legislatures were handed over to the right wing. It was the vacuum at the top of the Democratic Party that created the giant sucking sound of political influence being blown away.

As Ronald Reagan understood best, you can fight for the center only by arguing from the outside. The battle for American centrists cannot be won by pretending to be one of them. Rather, American centrism is a philosophy of moderation and inaction, standing for nothing and hoping that everything goes well enough to avoid making any decisions.

Democratic centrists are people who wave with the latest political wind, measured by an ever-present poll. They stand on no principles except the Machiavellian principle of maintaining political power.

Centrism fails as a political philosophy because nobody, not even a centrist, believes in it. Most centrists in America are not ideologically stuck in the middle between the Democrats and Republicans. Indeed, it's becoming increasingly difficult to tell the difference between the procorporate policies of the Democratic Party and the procorporate policies of the Republican Party. Centrists in America are centrists because of their disillusionment with politics. Independence is a popular alternative to both political parties because the political establishment has been so widely corrupted. That's why Ross Perot and the Reform Party could so easily fill a void. The Reform Party was never a centrist party in Clinton's style of lurching to the middle on every issue; it was a magnet for people from a wide range of perspectives who had given up on politics.

American centrists are largely pragmatic progressives without strong ideological ties who have given up on politics. They generally believe in basic progressive ideas: racial and gender equality, the social safety net, investment in education, an end to corporate welfare and government corruption, and protection of our rights. But they don't trust any of the current political candidates. These centrists would support most aspects of an honest progressive program, but they don't believe it's possible.

WHY PROGRESSIVES NEED THIRD PARTIES

For decades, the far right of the Republican Party has exerted control by threatening to abandon any candidate who failed to accede to their ideological demands. By contrast, progressives have stood loyally behind centrist Democrats in order to block conservatives from taking over the government.

Considering the procorporate Democrats who have been elected and their conservative policies, it's not clear that the Republicans would be substantially worse. The unification of the two parties behind the rich and the powerful means that the gap between Republicans and Democrats is much harder to discern. From the North American Free Trade Association (NAFTA) to welfare reform to the military, the difference between conservative Republicans and centrist Democrats is increasingly difficult to find.

Third-party candidates such as Ralph Nader won't win the presidency. But progressive candidates can help broaden the public debate to include progressive ideas. Except in a handful of states during a tight election, it usually doesn't matter if a substantial minority of progressives vote for a third party. It's far more important to give apathetic voters a reason to vote.

Until Democrats respect their progressive voters more than their corporate donors, third parties will be a necessity. This doesn't mean that the left must abandon the Democratic Party. To the contrary, third parties are a mechanism for increasing progressive influence within the Democratic Party. By creating an active base of voters who have an alternative to the two-party system, leftists will provide an incentive for the Democrats to move toward the progressive mainstream. If the Democrats turn centrist in order to attract conservative votes, they will lose a substantial part of their progressive base, which is a majority of the American people. Punishing the conservatives who have taken control of the Democratic Party is the only way to force change. By adopting progressive positions, Democrats can finally establish themselves as the majority party.

That's why American centrists have no respect for candidates who try to walk down the middle of the road. Centrists would much rather follow someone who believes in something than a candidate who always appeals to the least common political denominator. To wit: Ronald Reagan was widely liked and respected by a large part of the American people, even though his conservative policies ran counter to the prevailing will.

It's precisely this point that Bill Clinton, for all his intelligence, never understood. Clinton hinted to progressives that he would be a Trojan Horse of the left. He would enter the White House riding a centrist car, wearing the mask of moderation. Once inside, he would triumphantly lead the country to the promised land of leftist liberation. The joyous people, their eyes opened to the promise of progressivism, would embrace a second term.

Like anyone else who ever trusted Clinton, progressives were terribly disappointed. Clinton won by abandoning any principle when faced with tough resistance. He was the type of leader who had to ask where the people were going so that he could run ahead and lead them.

Because Clinton had never argued for progressive ideas, he

had no experience fighting on their behalf. Not surprisingly, he turned tail and ran for the center at the first sign of the inevitable opposition to some of his tamest proposals.

The first, and last, progressive proposal was to allow gays in the military, which Clinton planned to order immediately upon taking office. Out of all the progressive positions to take, defending gays and lesbians as one's first presidential initiative belongs in the category of noble but stupid. A genuine strategist for the left would have urged an extensive program mixing highly popular progressive proposals with a few unpopular ones. But Clinton was neither a strategist nor a progressive, and gays in the military must have seemed like the perfect issue: if he succeeded, progressives would hail his triumph. If he failed, he could blame the progressive ideology and abandon it completely for the rest of his administration—which is precisely what happened. Clinton was tossing out a sacrificial fag, waiting to see if anyone would bash him. To no one's surprise, the Republicans (and a few conservative Democrats such as Sam Nunn) jumped on the issue with glee.

Rather than gain some respect among everyone by fighting for his beliefs, Clinton instead made his predictable retreat to the center, offering "don't ask, don't tell" as a compromise proposal. In the end, Clinton's centrism failed miserably, as "don't ask, don't tell" became the slogan of a renewed military witch-hunt. The second great mistake of the Clinton administration was health care. Having dismissed progressivism forever with his blundering approach on a small issue, Clinton was determined to prove that his philosophy of centrism could produce far greater accomplishments than progressives imagined possible. National health care was one of those key issues.

Once again, though, Clinton's approach was doomed from the start. A progressive health care plan, pursued aggressively with a good strategy, might have succeeded—at the very least, it would have set the stage for later reforms as the managed care revolution reached into the hospitals and the doctors' offices.

But Clinton rejected the progressive single-payer approach and instead offered a confusing and complicated scheme that was attacked for being ineffective, wasteful, bureaucratic, and conducive to rationing. In the end, all these things did happen—but under private managed care companies, who took the massive profits that progressives had wanted to use instead for covering the poor.

Throughout his administration, Clinton learned all the wrong lessons. His failure at health care only reinforced his conviction that the center must be bowed to. The media pundits who wouldn't discuss single-payer health care concluded that Clinton had stumbled because he pursued a "leftist" "big government" agenda, when it was the failure to do so that actually left him twisting in the wind without any allies and brought him down. For the rest of his time in office, Clinton not only avoided progressive policies, he avoided any policies of substance at all.

Clinton's centrism also failed on a political level, because Bill Clinton begot Speaker Newt Gingrich. Progressives can't blame Clinton for Gingrich's nasty personality or his far right views. But Gingrich became Speaker only because of Clinton's mistakes. In 1994, Clinton was too concerned about saving his own centrist skin to fight for Democrats who might work for his agenda (if he ever got one). Gingrich's rise to power was due primarily to a corrupt political system in which he could raise hundreds of millions of dollars, create a network of activists and donors using nonprofit groups in a tax fraud scheme, and press a far right agenda against the will of the American public.

Gingrich ultimately won because he was fighting an ideological battle without an opponent. The Republicans, well financed and finally united behind Gingrich, presented a juggernaut that could have been beaten only by showing the American people how dangerous their vision of the country was. Instead, the disorganized and divided Democrats had nothing to fight with. Their progressive core felt betrayed. Their president was working on his reelection campaign two years down the road, not the immediate right-wing danger. The reigning philosophy of centrism in the Democratic Party proved to be the final nail in the coffin. Gingrich won without having the national debate that would have destroyed him (and eventually did), considering the massive unpopularity of his views. The Republican Party was awarded Congress without a fight.

The main reason for Gingrich's downfall was that ironically enough, he became the protégé of Bill Clinton. Upon becoming Speaker, Gingrich tried to move to the center. He pushed his Contract with America, which mostly passed the House but went nowhere in the Senate, and then blundered badly along with his far right allies by shutting down the government.

Clinton might have stood for nothing but his own power, but he was a wonderful tactician. Refusing to back down when Gingrich sought control was an almost instinctive but crucial move. It was the only moment in the Clinton administration when the president stood resolutely and publicly against the right without wavering. The Democrats must be taught this lesson: it was the most popular move Bill Clinton ever made.

The difference between Gingrich and Clinton is that Gingrich was genuinely incompetent at governing, whereas Clinton was simply unwilling or unable to push a progressive agenda. If he wished, Clinton could brilliantly thwart the attempts by his opponents to gain power. But Clinton could never lead an effective attack or promote any significant change because he was trapped in the failed philosophy of centrism. Gingrich, on the other hand, was, by his disposition and his lack of charisma, a terrible failure as a centrist. When Gingrich tried to match Clinton step for step on Clinton's centrist turf, he succeeded only in alienating both his core supporters and the centrists he hoped to convert to his cause.

THE CLASS DISTORTION IN AMERICAN ELECTIONS

The common assumption that we live in a full-fledged democracy must be questioned when examining the identity of voters. Whereas two-thirds of Americans who earn more than $50,000 vote, only one-third of Americans who earn less than $10,000 vote. The result is a class distortion in our democracy. Politicians seeking out likely voters will try to appeal to the upper-middle class, not the poor. The reason for this class difference is not that the poor have fewer civic concerns than the rich. The reason is money. The poor (and even well-off progressives) have fewer reasons to vote when the candidates available rarely serve their interests. And because politicians follow the money more often than the public will, the poor often end up choosing apathy rather than guessing which of two evils is the lesser one.

The class distortion even extends to polls, which usually screen for "likely voters." Since the poor are less likely to vote (and many immigrants are not allowed to vote), any poll that seeks to predict an election intentionally biases the survey results to favor the views of the wealthiest Americans. A liberal may be clearly preferred by a majority of Americans, but the conservative might win the polls—and the election.

Pundits typically are happy to blame nonvoters for their apathy. But to progressives, these "lost" voters are an opportunity to transform American politics. If a progressive candidate can ever be established, the "lost" generation of voters will provide the winning margin. As voter registration (and perhaps one day, voting itself) becomes easier, the progressive movement is likely to win—that's why Republicans have fought to stop motor voter registration laws and similar efforts to encourage voting.

(continued)

The "lost" voters can swing future elections to progressive causes, which is one reason that it's important to create viable progressive parties. Even if a progressive party such as the Greens never wins, it will recruit some of these disillusioned voters and raise progressive issues. The Democrats will move to the left in order to keep its base, and as a result these progressive candidates will attract even more of the "lost" voters.

Clinton won all the battles, but he lost the war. He lost the chance at having a legacy. He even lost his soul, since no one believes anymore that he ever was a progressive or really believed in anything.

The public could respect Clinton when they thought he was a secret progressive hiding behind the mask of centrism. But when they found that once they burrowed deep into his ideology there was nothing but centrism, the people quickly lost interest in his agenda. When everything is the politics of symbolism, designed for nothing but popular appeal and inevitably vetted to ensure it does not exceed the narrow boundaries of centrism, the public ceases to care about the political process.

Clinton believed that taking a few popular positions would maintain his approval ratings. But he proved that approval and disapproval ceased to matter once they became the exclusive focus of his administration. Although the public approved of Clinton, for all of his philandering and lying, it no longer mattered because Clinton (unlike Reagan) never used his popularity to push for anything he believed in, since that would require believing in something beyond his ratings.

What Clinton blamed on a Republican Congress was really his own fault: he was an inactive, impotent president who couldn't propose anything of importance. The Clinton administration was simply incapable of imagining the possibility that progressive ideas could be popular. Newt Gingrich merely saved him the embarrassment of being unable to create an agenda beyond the handful of poll-driven centrist symbolic issues. Gingrich and the Republicans initiated virtually all the political activity in Washington after those disastrous first two years of the Clinton administration.

Centrism has failed as a political philosophy because it cannot challenge the status quo enough to offer a different vision of a better government. Centrism ebbs and flows with the polls, and therefore it cannot question the shaky foundation behind the dominant political views.

What centrists do not understand is that the popular will is dynamic. Centrism imagines the public as a cute puppy, waiting to be fed what it wants, and whining when it is disappointed. But the "public mind" is actually quite open to the force of arguments. Progressive ideas fail not because they are considered and rejected but because they rarely get the chance to be heard and effectively argued. Centrism shuts out the possibility of a progressive politics and turns it into a small number of poll-driven policies that never really explain or challenge a corrupt system of politics.

American centrism also goes by another name: neoliberalism. Neoliberalism (which more properly ought to be called *corporate liberalism*) has absorbed the Democratic Party almost completely under Bill Clinton and his centrist allies in the DLC. The mistake made by neoliberals such as Clinton is to assume that liberal ideas must be sacrificed to gain popular approval. The real reason, however, that liberalism is sacrificed under the neoliberal agenda in order to get money, not votes.

Pragmatic progressives must often accept compromises, but this doesn't mean they have to compromise their principles. Progressives can present their goals openly, even if the final policies do not go as far as is needed. The centrism offered by neoliberalism, by contrast, has no guiding principles. Neoliberalism gave the Democratic Party politics without a philosophy, fund-raising without an intellectual foundation, and power without a mission.

Until progressives can persuade the Democratic Party to recognize the failures of centrism, the left will be doomed to be a forgotten minority within a fading political party. Progressives offer the Democratic Party an opportunity to embrace a majority philosophy that can lead them back to power—and also give the Democratic Party a set of meaningful core principles.

Chapter 4

POLLS

The Circle of Lies

America has become a nation of polls. Once the campaign season gets rolling, you can't open a newspaper without getting slapped in the face by some inane poll, touted by some media corporation that has determined (using a poll) that readers prefer to see polls rather than actual news.

Many local TV newscasts and newspapers—and a huge number of web sites—have created "polls" to ask their audiences about a topic of the day. Infamous Clinton and Jesse Helms consultant Dick Morris has even linked up with a web site, vote.com, that exists for the sole purpose of "polling" visitors. These self-selected response "polls" are completely worthless, even by the lowly standards of the dismal science called polling. The response "polls" can tell you only the views of a small group of people dumb enough to waste their time filling out phony polls.

This doesn't mean that all polls are useless. Unfortunately, the popularity of polls reflects the fact that properly conducted, they can inform politicians about changes in support or how the public is responding to certain key political phrases. Polls can tell us that people support affirmative action and oppose racial preferences. That's useful information if you're choosing rhetoric, but it doesn't answer any questions about what public policy on race should be selected.

Serious pollsters don't actually believe they can know what the American people really think by using polls. Instead, polls have become tools of verbal manipulation and political profit. A politician takes a poll in order to find out how the public will react to a certain policy, in some cases even how the public is interpreting a particular phrase. The question is not what people really think but how the politician can secure victory in the next election.

I could list all the polls that show that Americans believe in progressive ideas. I believe Americans are progressive minded. There's just one problem: I don't believe in polls. I don't believe that the American media's obsession with polling has enlightened us about anything. I care about what people think, but I don't care how they respond to polls.

I've never participated in a poll, but I always wonder how people manage to answer. "Do you favor national health insurance?" some underpaid pollster's temp (without any health insurance) would ask me. I'd answer, "Probably, but it depends. How is the health insurance structured? Does everyone get covered? Who's making the money from it?"

"Do you want to cut taxes?" would be the next question. I'd answer, "It depends. Which taxes? How much? What programs will be cut? Can I lower some taxes but raise others?" And then the poor poll-taking temp would tell me I can answer only yes or no or don't know. I'm probably a don't know. Or maybe a knows-too-much.

Maybe that sounds arrogant, but I think most of the American people know too much. Their ideas are too complicated to be neatly summarized in a poll for the morning paper. Even Dan Quayle's ideas are too complicated to be neatly summarized in a poll. The problem with polls isn't the public's ignorance but the ignorance inherent in the medium of mainstream polling.

Polls can discern only an uneducated public's response to an issue they have heard and thought about very little. We ought to be concerned instead about how the public might react to an idea if it were given the time and opportunity to hear all sides and deeply explore an issue. Until people have a chance to hear progressive views, it's impossible to determine accurately to what extent they might agree with them. The widespread support in polls for many leftist attitudes, despite the near-total absence of progressive thinkers from the mainstream media, suggests that the left could persuade a strong majority of Americans if given half a chance. But all the polls in the world won't tell us the truth.

Polls are the foundation of sound bites. It's a vicious circle: you force people to make black-and-white, yes-or-no choices in a world that has not only shades of gray but colors too. Then you tell the politicians that people believe these narrow-minded concepts. So the politicians shift their messages into sound bites that will generate the right poll results, and then pollsters take polls to test the sound bites, and people react to the sound bites, and on and on it goes. Polling, not television, has primarily fueled the rise of sound bite politics.

Marvelous, isn't it? The pollsters lie to the people about which political answers are the only worthwhile ones. The people, eager to please, lie about what they think. The pollsters lie to the politicians about what it means. The politicians lie to the people to please the polls. It's a circle of lies.

One is tempted to ask who thought of this system and have him cast off the edge of the flat world (which if you phrase the question correctly, a slim majority will tell you does, in fact, exist).

Polls appeal, perversely, to the notion that we are a democratic system that cares about people think. But it turns out that we don't actually care what people think because that would require too much time and money. So instead we care about how they respond. The poll thus is a cheap, efficient mechanism to look into the most shallow reaches of the American soul.

Polls have created a political system based on the instantaneous reaction and the ignorant opinion. Not only do the politicians use them to test every original thought (and a lot of unoriginal ones, too), but the media have also become consumed by the polling industry.

During election season, no self-respecting media conglomerate can last more than a few days without presenting the latest poll numbers and hauling in ponderous pundits to guess at the reasons that the numbers have fluctuated slightly since the previous poll on the previous day.

Candidates have even developed push polling, a technique in which a campaign worker pretends to be a pollster and then seeks to convince the wrong-answering respondent to change her mind (this allows candidates to "test" which words will convert people). Because people foolishly trust pollsters more than campaign hacks, they're more likely to stay on the phone for the message.

For what they spend on pollsters, news organizations could hire investigative reporters to do a serious report on the candidates' record on political bribery and other important issues. But that will never happen. Polls have the easy ring of firm truth. Polls arouse no controversy, whereas investigative journalism often does. And polls can be instantly converted into a cute pie chart for our *USA Today* media age.

Thus we learn which presidential candidate the American people prefer before any of them have bothered to mention what they represent, before most Americans even know their names. Most potential candidates are instantly dismissed as hopeless because they have no chance of raising money or gaining name recognition without media coverage, and the media refuse to cover them when the public doesn't know who they are—which, of course, will never happen without the media coverage. The circle of lies makes it virtually impossible for most candidates to be heard.

The word *poll*, of course, is an outright theft of the real "poll"—you know, the one people used to go to in order to vote for their favorite candidates, in the good old days before Mr. Gallup would tell you who was going to win a year before it happened. Now, the expression "going to the polls" refers to the biannual trek of politicians to pollsters who, like modern-day oracles, can tell them the future.

Polls, like the election cycle, are breaking out of even these limitations. Since committed candidates are constantly raising money to run for their next office, they have to take constant polls in order to find out how they must suck up to the public in the most effective way (without, of course, offending their big donors who provide the money to run the television spots that allow the politicians to suck up to the people without the tiresome task of actually meeting them).

Pollsters would like to have you think that like weather forecasters, the science of polling has dramatically improved in recent years. But meteorologists are studying real science, whereas pollsters are dealing with the most complex of all phenomena, human behavior. Meteorologists actually examine the intricate interactions of weather phenomena, while pollsters offer multiple-choice (or, more often, true/false) answers to the most important questions of our day.

At least they claim to be important. It's precisely because polls are so ridiculously bad at telling us what people truly believe that most pollsters ask the simple questions: what candidate do you support? Do you have a positive or negative impression of the president?

Even this kind of question befuddles me. My impression of the president usually is a complicated mix of revulsion, disgust, pity, reluctant admiration on certain issues, disappointment, and a few sex jokes. Positive and negative can't begin to explain my view of politics.

My advice, if you ever are asked to participate in a poll, is to lie obsessively. Tell them you're supporting "Bozo the Clown" for Congress—it's usually not far from the truth. Say "Dan Quayle would make a good president" while laughing hysterically. Inform the pollster's temp that you believe Washington, D.C., is about to be sucked into a black hole and disappear into an alternative universe. Or repeatedly ask, "What idiot came up with that question?"

Not that it will do any good. The advantage for pollsters is that if you ask one thousand people to respond to a stupid question, 95 percent of them will, and the pollsters will then claim to have achieved statistical significance.

The other key problem with polls, aside from their superficiality, is the fact that they are fixed in time. No one knows how the American public would respond to a question about health care if they were truly educated about the costs and human lives at stake, as opposed to glancing at a corporate-sponsored Harry-and-Louise commercial on their way to the bathroom. No one knows how the American public might react to a progressive agenda if it were adequately explained and promoted because nobody's ever been allowed to try.

Any argument that uses "most Americans believe" is not an argument; it's an admission of an inability to provide any intellectual basis for an argument. The "popular will" becomes an easy substitute for logic. Polls remain powerful because of the ignorance of everyone involved. Because a progressive agenda depends on an informed public thinking beyond sound bites, the American obsession with polling is one of the greatest barriers that leftists face.

THE FROZEN PIZZA POLLS

The greatest polls ever made appeared on documentary humorist Michael Moore's *TV Nation* program. These are real polls—phone surveys of randomly selected Americans. But the questions asked reveal far more about the American character than the typical polls:

Sixty-five percent of all Americans believe that frozen pizza will never be any good and there's nothing science can do about it.

Sixteen percent of Perot voters believe that "if dolphins were really smart, they could get out of those nets."

Seventy percent of American women have never had an emotionally satisfying relationship with a Republican.

Sixty-two percent of Americans believe that a trip to a major theme park is more culturally enriching than a trip to the Reagan Library.

Thirty-nine percent of Americans believe that guns are not "as dangerous as they say."

Twenty-nine percent of Americans believe that Elvis was right to shoot TV sets.

Twenty-six percent of those who possess a firearm believe that the Second Amendment protects their right to buy explosive fertilizer.

Sixty percent of Americans say that if they could push a button that would make Larry King disappear, they would "keep pushing it and not stop."

Eleven percent of people who have tried Prozac would like to see Dan Quayle make a comeback because "Al Gore just isn't funny enough."

Chapter 5

THE POLITICS OF MONEY

Campaign Financing and One Dollar, One Vote

America is a capitalist country, and nothing is more capitalist than its elections. Under a system in which politicians can be bought and sold like Frosted Flakes, progressive ideas are doomed to irrelevance. When cold cash determines political influence, those without big money can't pay the entrance fee to power.

The best rhetoric in the world can't persuade Congress if politicians will listen only to the sound of money. That's why campaign finance reform must be a top priority for all progressives. This isn't just another important issue; it's the foundation for changing how every progressive issue gets heard in Washington and around the country.

Legalized Bribery

Let's say that Joe Smith is a cop in your neighborhood. Because you like him and what he stands for (law and order, that sort of thing), you give him $1,000. You certainly hope he keeps an eye out for your home, car, family, and business. Who knows? If you ever get into trouble or your kid does, you figure Joe will be willing to help you out. After all, if you give a guy $1,000, you expect something for it, right?

The same goes for Jack Jones, the judge in your town. He gets $1,000 from you, even though you've never actually talked to him. But you figure that someday (keep those fingers crossed) you might end up in his courtroom, and it can't hurt to give the judge a big pile of money.

Most people would call this bribery. After all, if we let people hand out huge amounts of cash to law enforcement officials, how can we trust our criminal justice system? How can we expect them to treat everyone equally when they get extra cash from certain folks? That's why we pass laws to prohibit handing cash to the people who enforce the law.

But sometimes this bribery is completely legal—if Joe and Jack are running for elected office. If Officer Smith is trying to become Congressman Smith, that $1,000 bribe is perfectly legal. Of course, you can't slip him a wad of cash; you have to donate a check to his campaign. But he can't get the job without a lot of donations, and the job gives him lots of perks, a nice salary, good pension, lifetime job as a lobbyist, and something a lot of people want—power. Representative Smith is grateful.

For most of us, a grateful member of Congress isn't really worth that much. Unlike the cop who doesn't give you a ticket, Congressman Smith can't actually do a lot to help the average citizen. But now let's say that you're a multibillionaire financier or a huge corporation. You don't give a damn about Officer

Smith (after all, you have a private security force), but Congressman Smith is like your neighborhood cop. He helps pass the laws regulating how you operate, what taxes you pay, what government subsidies you get. And if a few thousand dollars from you and your employees and your relatives and your golfing buddies give Representative Smith a warm feeling about you and your legislative requests, hey, you give a guy lots of money, and you have the right to expect something for it, right?

Unlike Officer Smith or Judge Jones, your congressman can actually decide on the laws across the entire country. If a few thousand dollars aren't enough because of the rising Cost of Bribery Index, you can always give more substantial amounts of soft money to Representative Smith's buddies in the Democratic Party (or was it the Republicans? Sometimes it's difficult to tell the difference) and tell them to use it on his behalf and make sure he knows where it's coming from. All perfectly legal.

Maybe you can even have Representative Smith intervene on your behalf with a federal agency or hold hearings on a topic of deep importance to him. A donor once sent Newt Gingrich a letter crudely demanding his help with the EPA (U.S. Environmental Protection Agency) and listing all the thousands of dollars he'd given to Newt's "nonprofit" organizations designed to promote Gingrich and recruit Republican activists. Newt immediately wrote to the EPA, asking them to get off this lovely donor's ass (he used more congressional language, but the message was the same). The really proper rich people, of course, don't send embarrassing letters—their lobbyists have closed-door meetings and lunches at which the donations never have to be brought up, and the stakes are much higher. Sometimes our busy representatives remove this layer of bureaucracy and simply invite the corporate lobbyists to write the legislation themselves, as happened with the 1995 Telecommunications Act.

The notion that it's unconstitutional to stop campaign bribery is absurd. Although the First Amendment protects freedom of speech, it's impossible to imagine how "free speech" could include handing out $20 bills to voters (which is how Benjamin Harrison defeated Grover Cleveland for president in 1888) or giving far larger sums to politicians. Founding Father James Madison once lost his legislative seat because he refused to follow Virginia's political tradition of bribing voters with free alcohol, but he never repeated the mistake. Political corruption is not new, but it has been transformed. The decline of political machines and the growth in population have made broadcast advertising the key to winning elections, and money is the fuel that drives a campaign. However helpless Madison (the author of the First Amendment) might have felt about the American tradition of bribery, he never would have imagined that a law outlawing this corrupting practice was a violation of the Bill of Rights.

The corruption of American politics is proceeding at a historic pace. During the 2000 election, the Democratic and Republican Party committees took in more than $410 million in soft money donations, far above the $260 million in 1996 and five times the sum raised in 1992.

Money helps give wealthy special-interest groups plenty of special power in Washington. For example, Archer Daniels Midland is one of the world's leading recipients of corporate welfare thanks to huge farm subsidies, ethanol tax breaks, and sugar tariffs. It's no coincidence that ADM gave $700,000 to congressional candidates between 1993 and 1999 and more than $1.3 million in soft money to both parties between 1995 and 1999. While ADM was fixing prices to steal billions from farmers and consumers (for which it pleaded guilty and paid a record $100 million fine), the company continued to receive $83.5 million a year in federal contracts.

Public Campaign issued a report in May 2000 showing how the money behind right-wing causes has influenced legislation. From 1997 to 1999, the National Rifle Association (NRA) and other groups opposing gun control gave $3.5 million to federal candidates and parties and paid out $2.3 million in TV commercials and independent expenditures. By contrast, the groups supporting gun control gave $235,000 and spent $22,000 in independent expenditures. The NRA and friends outspent the other side by a ratio of nearly 23 to 1.

The gun groups know how to reward their supporters with massive amounts of cash. The votes on the May 1999 legislation to regulate the sale of weapons at gun shows reveal how much the NRA influences the process. The senators who supported the NRA position received an average of $23,340; the ones who opposed the NRA had received only $815 on average (and this number was inflated by the $30,000 given to Illinois Senator Peter Fitzgerald, who supported the gun control measures but was less likely to support gun control than his liberal opponent—without Fitzgerald, the average was less than $57). In the House, the average NRA supporter got $11,195, while the opponents of the free flow of weapons at gun shows received an average of only $355.

Since 1997, many other destructive industries have used money to stave off congressional action. The tobacco industry gave at least $2.1 million to stop further regulation of cigarette companies. The alcohol industry gave $7.9 million to prevent stricter enforcement of drunk-driving laws. The pesticide industry gave $1.6 million, mostly to House Agriculture Committee members, to stop regulation of chemicals potentially hazardous to children. Representative Charles Stenholm (D-Tex.), who has received more than $250,000 from the pesticide companies between 1991 and 1998, helped lead the fight against a possible EPA ban on organophosphates because of the hazards these chemicals pose to children.

This industry money distorts the debate in Congress because no well-financed opponents are giving money to support candidates on the other side. The amount of money made making guns, alcohol, cigarettes, and pesticides is so enormous that a few million dollars (not counting the substantial amount of lobbying by these groups) is considered a bargain to stave off legislation that might threaten their large profit margins.

WHY FULL DISCLOSURE ISN'T ENOUGH

Because public support for reforming the American campaign finance system is so enormous, conservatives can't openly oppose the idea of stopping political bribery. So one of the favorite tactics of the right is to argue for the "full disclosure" of donations. According to this compromise approach, it's the secrecy, not the money, that corrupts American politics.

The full disclosure of legalized bribery won't help when corruption is widespread. After all, if every politician is doing it, how can the voters choose an honest candidate?

Full disclosure also depends on competitive media that are willing to inform the public about acts of bribery. If a corporation that owns the only newspaper and most of the radio and TV stations in a city also gives money to a politician, full disclosure won't matter. When the media are corrupted by big money, how can anyone trust them to oppose the interests of their corporate owners and advertisers?

Full disclosure is only the first step toward creating an honest and fair political system and requires a ban on bribery by limiting political donations to small gifts from individuals, with public financing to support a just system.

Public Campaign (www.publiccampaign.org) argues for Clean Money Campaign Reform, using public money to finance candidates who agree to accept strict spending limit and forgo private contributions. Reform is unlikely, however, because campaign money keeps the status quo in power. In 1998, 395 of 402 members of the House of Representatives ran for reelection and won—a reelection rate of more than 98 percent. So long as the vast majority of Congress profit from their support for guns, tobacco, alcohol, pesticides, and other industries, they won't support any efforts to level the political playing field and turn "one dollar, one vote" back to the democratic principle of "one person, one vote."

In many ways, the Democrats are a more corrupt party than the Republicans, because corporations buy influence in Washington in two ways: first, by giving large amounts of money to candidates who agree with their views (primarily Republicans) in order to help them get elected and, second, by giving large amounts of money to ambivalent candidates (primarily Democrats) to persuade them to support procorporate positions. While most Republicans are simply getting paid to vote their consciences, many Democrats are actively selling out in order to get the money they need for reelection.

Johnny Chung gave more than $300,000 to the Democratic National Committee in order to get access to the White House fifty-seven times. Yet the only reason that this particular scandal made the news was because Chung was funneling money from Chinese businessmen and government officials, which would be illegal. The more important fact that Chung was buying access to politicians barely qualified as news, since the habit is so widespread.

The attitude in the press toward the Chinese funding scandal seemed to be that sure, people are always bribing elected officials, but at least it's usually Americans doing the bribing. Why should the average American care whether it's big American corporations or big Chinese corporations or even the Chinese government that is responsible for corrupting their elected officials? None of them has the interests of the American public in mind.

Clearly, the Clinton administration's spineless policy on China was determined by the huge donations from American companies who wanted a piece of that lucrative market, not a small amount of money funneled by China, whose influence probably wasn't even made clear to Clinton administration officials. Multinational corporations that regularly violate human rights in their sweatshops are hardly likely to want a human rights policy enforced against China's totalitarian government.

Because the politicians attacking the Clinton administration's illegal money-grab from China are even more dependent on political bribery from large corporations and influential PACs, the fundamental problem of campaign financing never was raised.

The amount of money at stake is enormous. According to a Public Citizen report, "Delivering for Dollars," from 1995 to 1999, three national Republican fund-raising committees took in $30 million in soft money from managed care, casino gambling, and tobacco interests (Democratic committees collected $11 million). Not surprisingly, Senate Majority Leader Trent Lott (R-Miss.) and Senate campaign committee chief Mitch McConnell (R-Ky.) were the leaders in the Senate at stopping restrictions on soft money donations, but they also were responsible for seeking these gifts. Lott and McConnell were leaders in promoting the legislative interests of these corporations—stopping proposed laws to remove a tax deduction on gambling losses, pushing a $316 million tax break for the gambling industry, stopping strong "patients' rights" bills, and killing the McCain tobacco control bill.

Nuclear industry groups in the Nuclear Energy Institute (NEI) gave almost $15.5 million dollars to incumbent members of Congress in the 1998 election cycle. Their goal is to make taxpayers pay for the disposal of nuclear waste, including a bill to promote the transport of dangerous waste through populated areas 100,000 times in the next thirty years.

The system of legalized bribery makes it impossible to imagine that any serious progressive work can be accomplished when the procorporate side is packed with money and the propublic side can never keep up with the Benjamins—the millions of $100 bills that get tossed around in Congress.

Campaign Finance Spending Limits

Conservatives (who stand to lose most of the influence their money can buy if reforms are passed) often argue that the current financial limits are out of date. Inflation has reduced that $1,000 (in 1974 dollars) limit to only $300 in buying power today. The anti-reform people reason that if the limits were raised, candidates could spend far less time fund-raising, and challengers would be able to compete with incumbents. These speculations are completely wrong. Political candidates do not seek a set level of funding—rather, they compete with their opponents. Since higher limits allow all candidates to get more money, it will only increase the stakes and enhance the influence of big money on American politics.

Anyone familiar with fund-raising knows that big donations don't greatly reduce the time spent seeking money. The candidates will not spend less time on fund-raising if limits are lifted; they'll simply concentrate their time on the wealthiest individuals. The assumption that the $1,000 limit benefits incumbents also is wrong. Incumbents get the largest share of donations because of corporate PACs (which have a higher $5,000 limit and no overall limit). The only way that removing donation limits could reduce the time candidates spend seeking money would be if a few millionaires donated huge amounts to campaigns—but that would increase the danger of political corruption.

Lower, not higher, spending limits are needed because the 1974 spending limits underestimated the power of money. The designers of the law never imagined that political donors would coordinate their activities and invent PACs at every turn. Nor did the designers of the law imagine that millions of dollars in soft money would be used by political parties to protect incumbents and prevent political change.

The solution to the problem of political bribery is easy: ban soft money, tighten spending limits, and put politicians and donors in jail whenever favors are exchanged for money. Unfortunately, the politicians won't easily end the system that keeps them in power, despite the huge popular support for stopping corruption in both parties (proven by Republican John McCain's nearly successful run for president with campaign finance reform as the driving issue).

Our government, from the local mayor to the president of the United States, listens to a rich donor far more often than it pays attention to a poor constituent. Since 81 percent of the donors to congressional elections earn more than $100,000 a year, political influence ends up being wielded most often by the wealthiest people in America.

While pundits worry that investigations of sex scandals and questions about drug use will prevent excellent candidates from seeking public office, it never occurs to them that the American political system of institutionalized bribery discourages many more candidates who could be devoted and honest public servants. We may argue about whether a lying adulterer makes the best president; but surely we all would prefer to have candidates who refuse to exchange campaign donations for political influence.

Unfortunately, the campaign finance system discourages almost everyone with a strong sense of integrity from seeking office—and makes it virtually impossible for the few exceptions to win. Our politicians often are not chosen for their political abilities but for their fund-raising skills. The result, predictably, is an alarming decline in integrity and growing corporate influence over our political system. The result, also predictably, is an alarming increase in apathy among our citizens.

Because running for public office requires enormous amounts of money rather than simply dedication and good ideas, an entire generation is giving up on politics. We have replaced the old political machines with money machines, and the result has been an even less democratic system.

Conservatives are fond of pointing out that America spends more money every year on yogurt than on campaigns. But only a few hundred people run for federal office every year, usually in noncompetitive elections. If a few hundred people ate all the yogurt in America, we'd probably consider their consumption excessive.

Stopping Political Bribery

One of the most common arguments against campaign finance reform is that the spending limits imposed in the 1970s haven't stopped the massive increase in campaign money. Imagine if your doctor took that approach: "Well, we had an antibiotic that seemed to cure that disease, but when a resistance to it developed, we just gave up." Obviously the cure for the disease of political bribery is to keep refining the restrictions until we succeed.

The first step is a ban on "soft money," the unlimited contributions to the political parties that enable them to illegally finance their candidates. During the 2000 presidential election, the Republican and the Democratic Parties actually spent more on TV commercials than on their (publicly financed) candidates.

Prohibiting those $100,000 gifts would make it almost impossible to buy influence.

The second step is to ban contributions from corporations, which are already prohibited by law from giving money to political candidates. Unfortunately, corporations can easily avoid the ban by creating a political action committee (PAC). By banning corporate and trade association donations to PACs and limiting these special-interest PACs to the same $1,000 per candidate cap (and $5,000 maximum overall) imposed on individuals, corporations would be unable to buy direct influence. Leading members of Congress who run unopposed would also be unable to raise huge amounts of money to distribute to their favorite candidates in order to maintain party discipline.

The inevitable consequence of banning soft money and corporate donations would be an onslaught of "independent" advertisements, which happens when a corporation, PAC, or union runs its own ads on behalf of a candidate rather than giving the money to that candidate. As long as the source of the "independent" ads is clearly identified and they are not coordinated with a campaign, these endorsement ads, like endorsements from newspapers, may be very difficult to regulate. But "independent" ads don't pose the same threat of corruption as soft money or PACs because they can't be hidden from the public eye. A soft money and corporate money ban would weaken the ability of political parties—and the corporations who give them so much money—to impose their will on Congress. Currently, all the money concentrated at the top enables a party to control the political debate by choosing the commercials and the candidates who will be supported.

Ideally, a ban on billionaires' giving huge sums of money to their own campaigns should be passed again, in the hope that the U.S. Supreme Court will take a more reasonable position on the topic than it did a quarter century ago. Even with this large exception, American political campaigns can be cleaned up. Public financing of campaigns is essential, but it should be much easier—along with FCC rules forcing broadcast stations to provide free time for candidates—after soft money and corporate donations are killed. Once the source of endless money from the rich is cut off, most politicians will be anxious to prevent billionaires like Ross Perot and Steve Forbes from gaining a financial advantage.

Those who argue that campaign donations are a form of free speech rather than bribery must be either hopelessly naive or eternally cynical. They claim that it's better to finance elections privately through campaign donations. Still, I don't think they go far enough. If preventing public funding of campaigns is so important, why ignore the huge public expense of holding these elections and tabulating the results? Why not allow the highest bidder to pay for counting the votes? If a little cheating goes on, well, people have a right to expect something for the free speech, don't they?

In fact, if campaign donations are free speech, we could simplify the election process, reduce expenses, and promote free speech by simply electing the candidate who has the most money. One dollar could equal one vote, and the candidate who raised or borrowed the most money (or was rich enough to provide it) would win the election. Instead of spending the money on annoying TV commercials, the money raised could go to reduce the national debt.

The idea is amusing at first—until you realize that the results wouldn't be much different from the current political system. Money has become such an integral part of American elections that some people—including the Supreme Court and the American Civil Liberties Union (ACLU)—actually believe that limiting campaign spending would threaten our freedom.

Money is not free speech. The right to advocate the legalization of marijuana does not convey the right to purchase illegal drugs. An individual has the First Amendment right to declare that prostitution is a socially beneficial activity but will still be arrested for hiring a prostitute. It's odd to see conservatives who demand strict literalist interpretations of the Constitution suddenly turn around and demand a right to "freedom of money" that never appears in the Bill of Rights. James Madison certainly never intended to create a constitutional right to bribe politicians when he wrote the provision protecting "freedom of speech" in the First Amendment.

Unfortunately, the power of money that has corrupted all of American politics has had its greatest impact on the Democratic Party. Big corporate donations don't fundamentally alter the Republicans' ideology. In the Democratic Party, though, the battle between the corporate centrists and the liberal left has been decisively won by the people with the most money.

The reason that Democratic centrists have differed from their Republican counterparts for the past two decades is a complicated consequence of intraparty politics. Few people realize that the massive infusions of money into American politics have had only a small impact on the overall balance of Republican versus Democratic power, although the recent rise of Republicans in Congress can be attributed directly to money. While the parties can usually adapt to political circumstances, the more powerful effect on American politics occurs inside each party. Within the Democratic Party, corruption now reigns supreme as corporate centrists are favored by big donors.

The worst part of our corrupt campaign finance system is not the bribery but the apathy. The American people see a government that does not belong to them. When something is not yours, indifference is the consequence. The principal reason for public disgust with our government is the belief that our politicians are bought and sold by special interests with huge amounts of money. The only way to restore confidence in our government is not by sanctimonious, cliché-filled speeches urging greater public interest in elections but by altering the system that gives wealthy private interests so much control over our government.

Why explain the power of money in a book about progressive rhetoric? Because it's crucial to refute the assumption that progressive ideas have been rejected by the American people, an assumption based on the fact that progressive ideas are indeed largely ignored by American politicians. The debate over ideas is not an equal exchange of all possible thoughts. In a free market, intellectual arguments are as much a product as running shoes, with the most powerful marketing budgets determining which one is purchased in the marketplace.

The political debate in America generally reflects the ideas that are considered politically feasible in Congress; it's rare to hear a talk show discussion about a policy reform that will never have any hope of passage. Because so much of American intellectual activity revolves around the current political structure, the corporations that financially control American politics also influence intellectual life.

For running shoes and soda, the market can be an effective means to ensure competition. But policy debates and intellectual discussions cannot be run according to the free market. A serious intellectual approach requires considering a wide range of different views, regardless of the financial support for them. A just political system must return to the principle of one person, one vote that is demanded by the Constitution and end the rampant bribery in American political campaigns.

Chapter 6

THE MYTH OF THE LIBERAL MEDIA

How the Press Attacks Progressives

If they ever made a robot to replace Rush Limbaugh, the first words programmed into its processor would be an attack on the "liberal media." Limbaugh regularly complains about this "liberal bias" in the press while carefully exempting himself—one of the most widely heard radio talk show hosts in America—as a member of the media, for obvious reasons.

The accusation of a "liberal bias" in the media is believed because it is repeated so often. From Limbaugh and G. Gordon Liddy to Oliver North and a legion of lesser-known radio hosts, from the McLaughlin Group and Tony Snow to Thomas Sowell and the *Wall Street Journal* op-ed pages, "liberal media" have become the conservative pundit's favorite term. And because conservative voices outnumber progressive ones by a wide margin in the mainstream media, the cry of liberal bias usually goes unchallenged.

BIG BIRD VOTES REPUBLICAN: THE MYTH OF
LEFTIST PUBLIC BROADCASTING

Public broadcasting doesn't offer much of an alternative to the conservative bias of the mainstream media, despite the right's frequent attacks on the Public Broadcasting System. FAIR's studies in the 1980s and 1990s of the *NewsHour* on PBS, National Public Radio programs, and public TV programs found that establishment sources dominated what the public heard, even on these programs typically deemed to dig the deepest, on networks thought to be the most "liberal" of all. "You can hear just as many conservative voices in the commentary on NPR as liberal voices," public radio reporter Mara Liasson stated proudly on *Fox News Sunday* in 1997. Actually, you can hear many more voices of the establishment than progressive critics on public broadcasting.

A 1998 study by Vassar sociology professor William Haynes found that the public affairs programs on PBS showed none of the liberal bias imagined by critics. In fact, PBS has been dominated by right-wing talk shows (such as *Firing Line, McLaughlin Group, McLaughlin One on One*) and uncritical business programs (*Bloomberg Morning News, Morning* and *Nightly Business Reports, Wall Street Week*). Corporate representatives and Wall Street sources accounted for 35.3 percent of the appearances, followed closely by professionals (primarily mainstream journalists) and government officials (25.6 percent each). The general public and citizen activists accounted for only 10 percent of the sources, down from 18 percent in a similar study made six years earlier. Only 21.5 percent of all sources were women (down from 23.1 percent in 1992), with more than half appearing on just one program (*To the Contrary*).

If PBS and NPR are so protective of the establishment, why

does the far right usually single them out for attack? The reason is that public broadcasting offers the potential for a serious critique of the right-wing dominance of politics and information, even if it is falling short of this goal at the moment. Commercial broadcasting and print media are run by large conglomerates who can muzzle any journalists who get out of control; these companies can also be manipulated by advertisers and political interests if they are lax in the surveillance of their employees.

Public broadcasting, at least in theory, belongs to the public. If the people truly controlled PBS and NPR, progressive ideas would finally be given the opportunity to compete on a fairly equal basis in the marketplace of ideas that is now slanted so heavily to the right. That's why conservatives despise public broadcasting and want to cut budgets severely to the point that PBS and NPR are dependent on corporate advertising (such as the fifteen-second commercials on *Sesame Street* for antibiotics—"Pfizer brings parents the letter z—as in Zithromax") and procorporate foundations to provide them with money.

The constant attacks on a "liberal media" affect public opinion. A 1999 study by Republican pollster Frank Luntz found that 74 percent of Republicans think that most journalists are more liberal than they are and 7 percent think journalists share their ideology. That's hardly surprising. But even 47 percent of Democrats see journalists as more liberal than they are, with 16 percent sharing their ideology and 28 percent perceiving journalists as more conservative.

Yet evidence of a "liberal bias" in the media doesn't exist. These conservative claims are based on a few shoddy studies and dubious anecdotes. The overwhelming number of conservative voices in the press complaining about "liberal bias"—and the near absence of progressives attacking the more clear-cut examples of conservative bias—is proof by itself that the left, not the right, is shut out of the mainstream media. The right's relentless attacks on the media help explain why so many people imagine that the media are "liberal." In the war of ideas, the left is winning the battles on the ground but watching the media report them all as losses.

The Centrist Journalist

The evidence of "liberal" bias in the media cited by the right is a single Roper/Freedom Forum survey that supposedly found that 89 percent of Washington journalists voted for Clinton in 1992. Why did so many journalists vote for Clinton? First of all, it's not clear that they did, since the Roper/Freedom Forum survey oversampled journalists from very small papers and also had a tiny sample size. But the reasons that Clinton would appeal to the Washington press elite are clear: they were bored with Bush; Clinton was far more charismatic; Clinton was closer to them in age; and Clinton had grabbed the mantle of centrism that appealed to them—not to mention their self-interested desire to have a president likely to generate news, which Clinton certainly did. But there is no evidence that private voting by journalists had any effect on their reporting about Clinton.

In fact, 1992 was an aberration for the normally pro-Republican media. Bill Clinton is the only Democrat aside from Lyndon Johnson ever to receive a majority of the newspaper presidential endorsements since *Editor and Publisher* magazine began tabulating them in 1932. In 1992, Clinton received 149 endorsements, compared with 125 for Bush. But this was due to boredom with Bush (who received 79 percent of endorsements in 1988 versus Michael Dukakis); it was a personality bias, not a political bias.

Like Bush, Clinton's appeal to the media faded after four

years. In 1996, Clinton received only 65 endorsements, compared with 111 for the far-from-charismatic Bob Dole. In fact, judging by newspaper endorsements, the media have always been overwhelmingly pro-Republican. From Richard Nixon (78 percent in 1960, 81 percent in 1968, and 93 percent in 1972) to Gerald Ford (88 percent in 1976) and Ronald Reagan (73 percent in 1980 and 88 percent in 1984), Republicans have received most of the endorsements for president—far from the "liberal bias" imagined by the far right.

By ignoring the larger structure of the mass media conglomerates in America, conservatives are missing who holds the power in the press. It may be true that journalists (especially at the lower echelons) tend to be a little more liberal than the average American. The reason that these journalists might tend to be liberal is simple: they're paid so little. With by far the lowest starting salary of any professional occupation, young journalists are less inclined to support Republican prowealthy policies. Although conservatives are not excluded from journalism, well-educated right wingers tend to seek higher-paying professions.

This is true mostly of the lower echelon of beginning journalists. At the level of high-priced "star" journalism—the John McLaughlins, the George Wills, the David Brinkleys, the Ted Koppels—no one believes that the conservatives are suffering. Once journalists reach the highest tax bracket, their concerns about the poor become more distant. Moreover, many of the media "stars" aren't really journalists at all. From Tony Snow (the only Sunday morning talk show host with a clear ideological perspective as a former Bush speechwriter) to George Will to Matt Drudge, the most influential media voices come from the mouths of conservative advocates.

Celebrity journalists are also lured by the money offered them to speak at corporate gatherings and conventions. From Cokie Roberts to most of the McLaughlin Group, tens of thousands of dollars are available to "journalists" ready to speak to powerful lobbying groups and corporations. Of course, none of them reveal to the public that they've taken large sums of money from companies with a direct interest in the policies they discuss. Progressives critiquing capitalism aren't paid tens of thousands of dollars to talk to capitalists; celebrity journalists would never be invited to give a liberal slant on the world for a hefty price tag.

Even if these rich journalists turn out to have a few liberal sympathies buried deep in their heart, it doesn't matter: the media conglomerates who hire them are concerned only with seeing media products made at the lowest possible cost and offering the highest possible profits.

THE 1 PERCENT ADVERTISING TAX

The problem of government financing for public broadcasting has an easy solution: a 1 percent tax on all advertising in the for-profit media. The money would go into a fund for public broadcasting as well as public billboards, public community newspapers, and many other not-for-profit endeavors. The public would save much of the tax money currently allocated to public broadcasting, which in turn would be better insulated from political retaliation in the form of budget cuts. Small grants would be available to create non-profit newspapers, radio stations, and TV stations across the country. Certain forms of advertising that are particularly pernicious (say, tobacco or alcohol advertising) could have higher advertising taxes imposed in order to finance antidrug education advertising.

A 1 percent tax is so small that it would not drive any broadcasters out of business. In many media corporations, the profit margins approach 30 percent, so even if none of the 1 percent tax was passed on to advertisers, the impact on media company profits would be tiny.

Because an advertising tax would be imposed nationwide on all kinds of media (TV, radio, print, Internet, billboards, even direct mail to help subsidize nonprofit mailing rates), it would offer no advantages to any particular media. With more than $165 billion paid to the media in advertising in 1999 (and $249 billion projected by 2004), a 1 percent tax would soon raise more than $2 billion annually to support community voices.

The only barrier to an advertising tax is the power of the media companies, which are among the most influential in the world. Not only do politicians seek their large political donations, but also they fear the ability of the media to launch investigations, distort the news, and endorse opposing candidates. That's the main reason that most sales taxes exempt newspapers and sometimes magazines.

But a 1 percent advertising tax is eminently fair. If companies have to pay taxes on the office supplies they buy, why shouldn't they pay a much smaller tax on the advertising they purchase?

If an advertising tax isn't feasible, there are other ways to subsidize public media: creating a substantial annual "frequency tax" on for-profit radio and television stations, imposing state sales taxes on advertising, or putting a 90 percent limit on the tax deductibility of advertising expenses. As media companies are consolidating, the public's trust in the for-profit media is declining, and the need for genuine public media is growing. Finding an independent funding mechanism for community media is essential.

The Conservative Bias of the Media

If you want to understand the nature (or bias) of a car, you look at the people who run the auto industry and the people they hire to design cars. The people who assemble the car in the factories are essential but not important: the autoworkers don't change the cars; they only make them correctly or badly. If someone discovered that autoworkers like Porsches, it wouldn't make a bit of difference to the Escorts they actually make.

Of course, journalism is not quite like auto assembly, but the resemblance is far greater than journalists or the public likes to imagine. The media create a consumable product, carefully arranged and directed. Reporters do what they're told and write in a standardized, "objective" manner about the topics they're assigned to cover. Editors monitor their work. The bosses decide who gets hired and fired. Conservatives are quick to complain and apply heavy pressure at the first sign of a "liberal" tendency in any reporting.

Right wingers have been complaining about "liberal bias" for decades. They created organizations such as Accuracy in Media (AIM), the Media Research Center, and the American Enterprise Institute's Center for Media and Public Affairs to attack the mainstream press and promote conservative causes. The mainstream media are sensitive to the accusations of "liberal bias" and bend over backward to appease the far right. When I criticized Steven Brill, the founder of the centrist media criticism magazine *Brill's Content*, for employing right winger Frank Luntz to conduct a poll on media bias, Brill replied that he had chosen Luntz because "we get criticized for being too much on the left."

Investigative reporter Robert Parry, who worked at the Associated Press and *Newsweek*, noted that "mainstream journalists lived with a constant career dread of being labeled 'liberal.' To be so branded opened a journalist to relentless attack by well-funded right-wing media 'watchdog' groups and other conservative operatives. AIM, for example, succeeded in having *New York Times* reporter Raymond Bonner removed from his Central America beat after he wrote about massacres by U.S.-supported troops. Many years later, UN excavations found that his reports were completely accurate." On the rare occasions when the media reveal the truth, they almost inevitably face condem-nation from the far right for "liberal bias."

The money of the right wing buys more than just these well-financed "watchdog" groups to promote the myth of the liberal media. The conservative funding also finances right-wing think tanks such as the American Enterprise Institute, the Heritage Foundation, and the Cato Institute, which provide easy jobs for conservatives who produce the sound bites and op-eds to fill up the mainstream news stories and editorial pages. According to a study by Fairness and Accuracy in Reporting (FAIR), more than half the think tanks cited in the Lexis-Nexis database of media coverage each year are right leaning (51 percent in 1999). About one-third (35 percent in 1999) are centrist think tanks such as the Brookings Institution (which is headed by a Republican), but far fewer (13 percent in 1999) represent progressive perspec-tives. Because the ideology behind the conservative think tanks is rarely identified by reporters, the conservative bias of sources goes unnoticed. Although many progressive think tanks exist (including the Economic Policy Institute, the Center on Budget and Policy Priorities, and the World Policy Institute), media pro-fessionals don't like to use them.

Conservative think tanks usually have more money than pro-gressive ones, because the right is willing to serve wealthy cor-porate interests. Conservative pundits are often quite willing to sell their services. Former New York lieutenant governor Betsy McCaughey Ross wrote to the president of the Pharmaceutical Research and Manufacturers of America asking the lobbying group "to support my work at the Hudson Institute, because my writings on healthcare policy can make a substantial difference in public opinion and in the nation's capital. My track record proves it." As intellectuals for hire, the right offers journalists mouthpieces for corporate America with the veneer of neutral-ity provided under the guise of a think tank.

CORPORATE TELEVISION AND
FALSE CONTROVERSIES

In 1999, virtually every major newspaper printed the "revelation" that PBS stations using independent brokers had exchanged mailing lists with various political groups, including the Democratic Party and Bob Dole's 1996 presidential campaign. Nothing about it was illegal, and considering how much political bribery goes on in Washington without a single headline, the uproar over PBS mailing lists was extraordinary. A barter is not a bribe. The trading of mailing lists is a simple economic deal beneficial to all sides. The fact that PBS officials judged that Democrats might be more generous than Republicans is hardly a surprise given the right's anti-PBS rhetoric.

But PBS officials made the worst of all mistakes: they denied and apologized instead of defending the practice. "I'm sorry" is never a winning argument. Of course, PBS folks aren't necessarily interested in winning an argument: they want to avoid offending anyone in order to preserve the tiny remaining sliver of federal funding.

Oddly, while the thoroughly legal practice of donor list exchanges was publicly crucified, the illegal—but nevertheless commonplace—practice of running commercials on public television has received almost no media attention. Public stations often run thirty-second advertisements identical to those played on commercial television. Unfortunately for those money-grubbing PBS officials, it's illegal to run these commercials, and they've been ordered to pay fines for the violations—but the revenue from advertising nevertheless makes it profitable.

The reason that the media chose to focus on the mailing list story might have something to do with the fact that most newspapers are owned by media conglomerates that own television stations and networks competing with public broadcasting for viewers. The *Chicago Tribune*, for example, used the mailing list situation to editorialize for the elimination of all publicly subsidized broadcasting—without bothering to note that its own broadcast stations would benefit from the removal of nonprofit competitors. Nor are the commercial media likely to suggest that running ads threatens PBS's autonomy—after all, what would that say about the credibility of the advertising-saturated for-profit media?

The PBS scandals revealed the priorities of the mainstream media: when a perfectly legal and routine trade of donor lists was made public, the press turned it into a major scandal because it supposedly helped Democrats. But when PBS stations illegally run commercials and distort their programming to serve corporate interests, it's not considered news.

Public broadcasting is a target for the far right because it has the potential to counter the conservative biases in the mainstream media. Unfortunately for progressives, that potential hasn't been realized yet. Public radio and television, freed from the right-wing biases imposed by media conglomerate owners and advertisers, could provide a genuine alternative to the corporate media and reflect the progressive attitudes of the public that supposedly owns these stations.

The reason for excluding left-wing views isn't an aversion to radical ideas, for the most popular conservative think tank is the libertarian Cato Institute, which promotes many views far out of the mainstream. Nor are progressive think tanks excluded because of their own failure to contact journalists, since many left-leaning think tanks seek media coverage more aggressively than do the better-funded conservative think tanks. The main problem is that reporters seem to be biased toward presenting political debates as a battle between the right and the center. Because the left is excluded from American politics, it's also excluded from the American media.

Even if one focuses exclusively on what reporters think, instead of what they actually report, there is no evidence of a "liberal" bias. A major mistake in many "bias" polls is that they often include every reporter in America, regardless of their position and influence. A kid fresh out of college who covers high school sports for a suburban weekly might be more liberal than the CEO reading the paper, but who cares? Are descriptions of touchdowns and zone defense somehow distorted by a liberal slant? No, obviously the key players in the major media are the only ones whose personal views might conceivably matter.

In a 1996 Greenberg poll commissioned by FAIR, the views of Americans were compared with a more relevant group of journalists—the Washington press corps. The poll found that these journalists are overwhelmingly centrist, leaning to the left on social issues and to the right on economic issues. On social issues, 57 percent call themselves centrist, 30 percent left, and 9 percent right. On economic issues, 64 percent are centrist, 11 percent left, and 19 percent right. Not surprisingly, more than half these Washington journalists live in households earning more than $100,000 a year (only 5 percent make less than $50,000 a year). Considering that conservatism tends to increase as salaries grow, the Greenberg survey probably understates the right-wing leanings of the journalists at the very top of the Washington food chain.

The Greenberg survey numbers also understate the conservatism of the Washington media elite because the political self-perception of white (89 percent), male (66 percent) millionaire journalists usually is based on a comparison with the conservative politicians and lobbyists with whom they hobnob rather than with the ideas of the average American. Many journalists who went to college during the late 1960s like to imagine that they hold left-leaning sentiments, regardless of their actual views.

On most specific economic issues, Washington journalists are far to the right of the general public. When asked about their economic priorities, the press was three times as likely as the public was to put the protection of Medicare and Social Security against major cuts "toward the bottom of the list." The reporters were twice as likely as the public to make their "single highest priority" urging "reform" for entitlement programs by slowing the increase in spending. Only 24 percent of the journalists, compared with 62 percent of the American public, strongly agree that "too much power is concentrated in the hands of a few large companies."

Perhaps the biggest gap between the public and the press concerns trade. On the question of expanding the North American Free Trade Agreement (NAFTA), 44 percent of the public put this issue toward the bottom of their economic priorities, compared with only 8 percent of reporters. Unlike the right's unsubstantiated allegations of "liberal" bias, there's strong evidence that the media's conservative bias on NAFTA was reflected in the news coverage. A FAIR study of the *New York Times* and the *Washington Post* news coverage of NAFTA in 1993 found that treaty supporters were quoted three times as often as opponents, while the pro-NAFTA views in the *Washington Post* op-ed pages held a 7 to 1 edge over critical perspectives. "Everyone's agreed with this," declared George Will about free trade on *This Week with David Brinkley* in 1997. And he was correct. The media were overwhelmingly supportive of NAFTA, along with most politicians. Only the public was skeptical, even though the press gave them almost no critical information about the treaty. If this is how the most "liberal" of the "liberal" media treated a major political issue, imagine how the rest of the news is covered.

A few "limousine liberals" imagine themselves to be progressive minded, even though their reporting rarely suggests it. Not surprisingly, these faux liberals are proud to tell a pollster whom they voted for or to describe their liberal leanings. Meanwhile, conservative journalists (such as Brit Hume, head of Fox News) view themselves as centrists in the face of "liberal" colleagues. The conservatives don't want to be revealed as conservatives, and the "liberals" don't want to be revealed as centrists. The true test is what actually is reported.

On virtually every issue, journalists usually head straight to the government experts, conservative pundits, and corporate PR hacks, ignoring progressive voices. The 1996 Greenberg survey found that the groups that journalists "nearly always" consulted on economic issues were government officials (51 percent), business representatives (31 percent), think-tank analysts (17 percent), university academics (10 percent, who in the field of economics typically lean to the right), and Wall Street analysts (9 percent). By contrast, labor representatives (5 percent) and consumer advocates (5 percent) are far less likely than business representatives and their supporters to appear in these news stories. When reporters who support the status quo quote the representatives of the status quo, where could there be any "left-wing" bias?

The Business of the Media

The media is an enormous industry in America, employing huge numbers of people. Finding examples of "liberal" bias is not only unsurprising, it's inevitable, and the same is true for anecdotes of conservative bias. But no one has ever made a comprehensive examination of bias in the entire media, so anyone claiming to know the absolute truth about media bias in reporting is simply guessing. Just in looking at the structure of the mainstream media and the corporate influences on it, however, the argument for "liberal bias" is impossible to sustain.

Of course, one might wonder why the conservative media don't simply seek to make money by being more openly right wing. A few are: the Fox News Network was started by billionaire Rupert Murdoch and is run by Roger Ailes, the head of George Bush's 1988 campaign for president. Murdoch similarly bankrolls the right-wing *New York Post* (which loses $20 million a year) and the right-wing magazine, the *Weekly Standard*, to provide a far right alternative to the center-right mainstream media.

Murdoch also eliminated the BBC World Service Television from his Asian satellite network after the Chinese government objected. Murdoch's publishing company even paid the daughter of the Chinese leader Deng Xiaoping to write a biography of her father.

Several other explicitly conservative newspapers are published, such as the *Boston Herald* and the Moonie-owned *Washington Times*, while no leftist daily exists today in any major urban area. (These conservative papers are especially vulnerable to the influence of advertisers: In April 2000, Robin Washington, the consumer and transportation reporter for the *Boston Herald*, was demoted after being told that he could not report on the higher bank fees resulting from the Fleet–BankBoston merger, which involves a powerful *Herald* advertiser. Washington was then suspended without pay after he complained.)

Richard Mellon Scaife's fortune enables him to finance right-wing causes through his foundation (such as financing the *American Spectator* magazine) as well printing the conservative *Pittsburgh Tribune-Review*, which featured Christopher Ruddy's front-page anti-Clinton conspiracy theories that both Vince Foster and Commerce Secretary Ron Brown had been murdered.

There are good economic reasons that media conglomerates wish to avoid being labeled as conservative, even if their reporting generally is. Media corporations are in the business of making money, not ideology. A newspaper that explicitly tilts far to the right would alienate too many readers and create the opportunity for genuine progressive competition. Although newspaper subscribers and other news consumers tend to be wealthier and more conservative than the general population (in part because the absence of progressive media drives many people away from the news media altogether), news consumers are still more progressive at heart than the American political establishment, which is biased toward those who can attract enough donations to win an election.

Media conglomerates also have good economic reasons to avoid challenging the political establishment. During the debate over the 1995 Telecommunications Act, media conglomerates gave $2 million to politicians over a six-month period in an attempt at influence peddling. Not surprising, few reporters offered serious investigative reporting of their own company's attempt to buy favorable legislation, and as a result, this massive giveaway of tens of billions of dollars in public airwaves went largely unnoticed by the public.

The media sometimes offer more direct support: in April 2000, Timothy White, editor and publisher of the *San Francisco Examiner*, testified in court that he offered San Francisco Mayor Willie Brown favorable editorials in exchange for Brown's support of the newspaper's $660 million purchase of the *San Francisco Chronicle*, which was threatened by a federal antitrust investigation.

Even when there is no deal to trade editorials for political influence, the conventions of journalism clearly are biased toward this status quo, not toward liberalism. Journalists follow power. They assemble when the rich and the politically connected call press conferences. They quote elected officials and only rarely give equal time to their critics. Whereas a politician or a business leader can make the news by simply standing in front of summoned reporters or tossing out press releases, the left is forced to devote massive amounts of energy to hold protests or file lawsuits in order to get similar attention. Even then, the mainstream media often ignore or downplay huge public protests.

The amount of news media has greatly expanded in recent years, with the rise of numerous all-news cable networks and the expansion of local and primetime network newsmagazines. But the quality of news coverage—and the resources devoted to the news—has declined. These news programs work with formulas and a cycle of repeating the same news of the day over and over. Wall-to-wall crisis coverage of a natural disaster, a plane crash, or a bombing is overwhelming, but quality investigative reporting that challenges the conventional wisdom is badly lacking. Because progressives have remarkably little to contribute to the public understanding of a hurricane, a celebrity sex rumor, or a salacious murder trial, the structure of today's news programs ignores the left.

Unlike progressives, the conservatives also have the advantage of media exclusively devoted to their ideas: a cable news channel (Fox) that is explicitly to the right of the mainstream, numerous religious TV and radio networks that promote their causes without any of the "objectivity" inhibitions of the mainstream media, and many radio talk shows, led by Rush Limbaugh, that allow conservatives to push their values without opposition. The conservative media help spread the myth of liberal bias, since the mainstream media certainly do seem a little liberal when compared with Limbaugh.

Only in the realm of magazines, with high-quality products such as *Mother Jones, Harper's, The Nation, In These Times,* the *American Prospect,* and *Z Magazine,* have progressives competed effectively against the better-funded right-wing counterparts of the *National Review,* the *American Spectator,* and the *Weekly Standard.* But these progressive magazines tend to preach to the choir—although their investigative journalism is excellent, the information rarely reaches the mainstream public. While the far right concentrates on reaching the mainstream media, the left struggles to keep a few small magazines alive.

The big reason for this disparity is money. Conservative media have a lot more of it than progressives. It's probably not an astonishing revelation that big corporations tend to be run for corporate interests. This means that any progressive programs run up against corporate conservatism at the very top, where the key decisions are made. You don't get to be a vice-president at a media conglomerate by routinely promoting progressive programs that challenge the corporate interests that own your company. You don't get hired as middle management by disobeying the vice-president. And you don't get to be a reporter by violating these procorporate standards.

Nor are media owners simply passive profit takers. The people who run media corporations become directly involved in news issues. In 2000, several journalists resigned from a group of free community weekly newspapers in San Luis Obispo County, California, because the conservative owners prohibited "promoting the gay lifestyle or abortion" in their newspapers. The owners banned an announcement for the local meeting of Parents and Friends of Gays and Lesbians, along with any letters on the subject or any articles showing support for gay rights or prochoice positions. Even when owners do not intervene in day-to-day decisions, they still call the tune. They hire the people who hire the people who do not challenge the prevailing ideologies.

A 2000 survey of nearly 300 reporters and news executives by the Pew Research Center and the *Columbia Journalism Review* found that 41 percent of journalists purposely avoided pursuing a story or softened the tone of it in order to benefit the financial interests of their news corporation. Furthermore,

51 percent of local journalists and 30 percent of national journalists believed that the owners of their news corporations exerted at least some influence on decisions about which stories to cover. About 20 percent of the reporters said that they personally faced criticism or pressure from bosses after producing or writing something piece that was deemed damaging to their company's financial interests. A separate survey of members of Investigative Reporters and Editors (IRE) found that half of investigative reporters believe that newsworthy stories are often or sometimes ignored because they conflict with the news organization's economic interests.

As the number of major media companies dwindles to a handful, the opportunities for conflicts of interest escalate. In October 1998, ABC News president David Westin stopped an ABC News investigation of convicted pedophiles working at Disney's Magic Kingdom. In the name of synergy, positive coverage of sibling networks and companies is actively sought. During the debate over the telecommunications bill in 1995, cable owner Time-Warner's CNN refused to run an ad by long-distance phone companies claiming that cable TV rates would rise because of the bill.

WHY WE NEED PUBLIC BROADCASTING

Conservatives and libertarians argue that with the growth of cable television, public broadcasting is unnecessary. Who needs animal flicks when you've got the Discovery Channel? Why have cooking shows when there's the Food Channel? What does PBS need business programming for when CNBC and other channels are devoted to it? Why bother to run documentaries if the History Channel does it?

One reason is that for all the virtues of some channels, most of cable is a vast wasteland with bad TV reruns, lousy movies, and

---

(continued)

mediocre original programming. And for the millions of people without cable, PBS offers an adequate (and sometimes superior) substitute, providing quality programs on a range of topics.

Progressive may wonder whether all the conservative influences on PBS mean that it should be abandoned. But for all its flaws, public broadcasting produces many programs that can't be matched anywhere. The *NewsHour with Jim Lehrer* is far superior to the network news shows, despite its consistently proestablishment bias. *Frontline* is a vast improvement over NBC's hokey *Dateline* documentaries, despite *Frontline*'s increasingly centrist tendencies. *Morning Edition* and *All Things Considered* on public radio can't even be compared with the pathetic attempts at news ("traffic and weather on the eights") heard on commercial radio.

Because Americans are accustomed to free television and radio, pledge drives can never come close to producing the true value of the programming to people. The only way to pay for public broadcasting is to raise money from the public, and that's the only way to have at least one form of competing media free from the controls of advertisers and corporate donors. Only additional funding for public broadcasting can protect it from corporate influences.

The word *media* is a plural noun. But after a wave of mergers, monopolization, and homogenization in recent years, "the media" need to be considered a singular entity. The media not only act as our eyes and ears, they also help shape our thoughts by providing the information that tells us what we ought to think. Thus when we see an endless parade of crime stories on TV, we worry about an epidemic of criminal behavior, even though the statistics clearly show a sharp decline in crime. When we are allowed to listen to only the limited range of thought provided by the two political parties in America, people dismiss the possibility of a different political movement that has not been sold out to wealthy donors.

The news media could do a great service to this country by exposing corruption, promoting sound public policies, and truly informing the people. Instead, we are given a massive wave of garbage, heavily biased by the demands of ever-growing and intrusive corporate owners, advertisers wary of progressive voices, and an established media elite devoted to pacifying criticism rather than sparking controversy and opening people's minds to a diversity of ideas.

Today, newspapers no longer have readers; they have consumers. Television networks and radio stations no longer have viewers and listeners; they have desirable demographics. Most of all, most of the time, the news media do not tell us the truth about the world; they are a profession of employees serving their employers by producing innocuous words.

While conservatives frequently attack "liberal bias" among news reporters (despite the lack of evidence that their personal views are truly left wing or affect the reporting), the only place where biases are openly expressed is on the op-ed pages. Here conservatives dominate the debate of ideas. As presidential endorsements show, most newspapers lean to the right in their editorial perspective, and conservatives dominate syndicated columns. According to a 1999 survey by *Editor and Publisher* magazine, the leading syndicated columnists are right wingers. James Dobson, president of Focus on the Family, leads the pack by appearing in 550 papers, followed closely by fellow right wingers Cal Thomas, Robert Novak, and George Will, all of whose columns appear in more than 480 papers. Several other conservatives make the list of 250 or more papers, including Mona Charen, Thomas Sowell, Morton Kondracke, Joseph Perkins, and Ben Wattenberg. Meanwhile, the only liberals appearing in at least 250 newspapers are Ellen Goodman (425) and Molly Ivins (250+), along with the left-leaning Nat Hentoff (250), and centrists Art Buchwald (250+) and David Broder (300).

Conservatives also are able to express their ideas more openly on television. There is no liberal counterpart to John McLaughlin or William F. Buckley with a weekly program on PBS, nor a left-wing news network to counter the explicitly conservative Fox News Network, nor a leftist critiquing society with the freedom that John Stossel of *20/20* has on ABC.

Stossel is quite open about his right-wing bias: "I have come to believe that markets are magical and the best protectors of the consumer. It is my job to explain the beauties of the free market." Stossel reports not only on *20/20*, he also has a full-time staff to produce several "documentaries" a year on topics such as greed (which is good) and organic food (which is bad). Stossel regularly speaks to corporate clients for large fees and donates some of his fees to the conservative Palmer Chitester Fund that promotes—coincidentally enough—the *Stossel in the Classroom* program to push his free-market ideas in schools.

The problem with the media is not the presence of conservatives such as Stossel but the absence of contrary views. Leftists should not seek to silence Stossel, despite his one-sided programs and their questionable accuracy. Rather, it's the silencing of progressive voices that must be the greater concern; a bland centrism without critical voices from the left or the right would be no better than the status quo. The main problem is that a leftist version of Stossel would be fired almost immediately by his corporate bosses if an advertising boycott organized by the far right didn't get rid of him first. Conservatives such as Stossel create the opportunity for progressives to demand that the other side of the story must be heard.

Money for Nothing and Ideology for Free

Advertisers also have a tremendous influence over the media. Radio and TV are entirely financed by advertising. A newspaper such as the *Washington Post* costs about $2.25 to produce but only 25 cents to purchase—advertising makes up for the rest, along with a large profit margin. Anyone who imagines that advertisers have no control over the media is simply hallucinating. A media outlet devoted to opposing capitalism would find it impossible to get enough advertising to survive.

Even prestigious newspapers such as the *Los Angeles Times* are deeply entwined with their advertisers. The October 2, 1999, issue of the *Los Angeles Times Magazine* was devoted to the Staples Center, a new sports arena. While some readers may have wondered why an entire issue about an arena qualified as first-class journalism, the hidden answer could be found on the business side of the *Times*: the issue was part of a deal with the Staples Center to become a "founding partner" of the arena in exchange for $1.6 million a year in cash, free advertising, and $300,000 from the sharing the profits of a special editorial product—the Sunday magazine. The Staples Center profited from the newspaper's coverage of the Staples Center, a conflict of interest that revealed how far journalistic standards had sunk toward the bottom line.

This "profit-sharing" agreement was a product of *Times* publisher Kathryn Downing and Mark Willes, CEO and chairman of Times-Mirror, which owned the *Los Angeles Times* (Times-Mirror has since been purchased by the Tribune Company, thereby further consolidating the media but also dumping Willes and Downing). Willes had become publisher of the *Times* in 1997 and immediately set to work breaking down the "wall" between the editorial and advertising departments. Willes appointed general managers overseeing each section to maximize their commercial potential. The Staples Center fiasco that resulted in part from the demolished wall was protested by a petition signed by 300 reporters and editors at the *Times*.

An internal, independent study of the issue by a *Los Angeles Times* reporter found numerous examples of the wall between editorial content and advertising being destroyed. The *Book Review* editor, Steve Wasserman, noted: "From time to time, it has been suggested to me that we should pay more attention to books published by companies with big ad budgets." The *Los Angeles Times* had also created a weekly health section with "a soft focus not likely to offend advertisers." The wall had been falling for many years. In 1994, the *Times* had scrapped an entire print run of its food section because a major grocery store advertiser saw an advance copy and objected to the cover story on food safety; a new headline and photograph were substituted to avoid seeming too "alarmist." The controversy over the Staples Center was unusual only because so many journalists at a leading newspaper finally stood up and objected to a secret deal with a business partner. This occasion notwithstanding, the market forces that drive editorial content toward advertiser needs are encircling the media around the country.

Even when advertisers do not directly attempt to control the news, they change the direction of the media's audience. The principle of equality does not apply to media consumers. Advertisers care about reaching people who have money. A family that spends $100,000 a year buying goods is worth ten times as much to the average advertiser as a family that spends $10,000 a year. For some major newspaper advertisers—such as new car dealers, expensive department stores, or real estate agents—impoverished consumers are virtually worthless. Companies with products oriented toward a mass audience—fast food, soda, breakfast cereal—prefer to use TV entertainment programs rather than news-oriented media to reach their consumers.

As a result, media conglomerates skew their media products toward an upscale audience. A prolabor, progressive newspaper geared toward the racially diverse working poor is no longer considered viable in today's economic climate. Even if advertisers did not oppose the leftist editorial views of such a newspaper, they would oppose its demographics.

Conservatives benefit from having a demographic that appeals more to companies with big money. Rush Limbaugh dominates midday radio because he reaches an audience of housewives, retirees, salespeople, and business owners who get to decide what radio station is on—unlike most of the regular workers who couldn't listen to a progressive version of Rush even if one were available. Conservative radio shows also have the advantage of having wealthy, white listeners, who are strongly preferred by advertisers.

Because the media owners actively seek a wealthy audience and because the rich tend to be disproportionately conservative, there is an economic incentive to disregard progressive and dissenting views.

Even a supposedly "liberal" medium such as public broadcasting is heavily controlled by its advertisers (or "sponsors," since advertising is technically, but not actually, prohibited). National Public Radio has a daily *Business Report* but no *Labor Report*. When a producer attempted to create a labor-oriented public television show, the Public Broadcasting System refused to allow it on the grounds that funding from labor unions compromised its objectivity—even though numerous probusiness programs are sponsored by corporations.

Another form of advertising used by corporations and rightwing groups is the press release. Because so many journalists are either unwilling to do serious reporting or unable to do so because cost-cutting media corporations impose heavy workloads, the press relies on its own releases to fill its pages and determine its news stories. Since corporations and conservatives can afford massive public relations machines, they benefit from positive media coverage.

When a stray progressive idea reaches the mainstream, corporations have another mechanism of control: the lawsuit. Oprah Winfrey moved her talk show to Texas for six weeks to fight cattlemen who objected to a guest pointing out the dangers of mad cow disease and Oprah's subsequent promise not to eat another hamburger. All the media are now clearly aware that a story about the hazards of mad cow disease or American beef could prompt a lawsuit—and therefore it's difficult to find much investigative reporting on the topic in any of the many states where food disparagement (or "veggie libel") laws prohibit the media from freely reporting bad news about food. After all, not many journalists can take six weeks off work and spend millions of dollars defending themselves against a frivolous lawsuit.

When an institution as powerful as *60 Minutes* could be dissuaded from going after the tobacco companies for fear of lawsuits, imagine how smaller, less prestigious media react to the threat of legal action. In 1998, the *Cincinnati Inquirer* paid millions and offered a front-page apology to Chiquita Brands because of an investigative report exposing the company's business practices. Although a reporter had "illegally" been given access to the company's voice mails by one of its lawyers, nothing about the series was ever shown to be untrue—the newspaper was simply terrified that it would lose a lawsuit and be vulnerable to a huge judgment. Corporations commonly try to suppress progressive causes by filing lawsuits, which are called Strategic Lawsuits Against Public Participation (SLAPPs). Libel lawsuits are the SLAPPs targeted against media coverage. The fact that very few of these suits hold up in court on final appeal doesn't reduce their power to intimidate, since the goal is to force settlements and to pressure the media to avoid investigative reporting.

Truth at War: Journalists and the Military

During peacetime, the media rarely challenge political authority. But when war begins, the critical role of the press disappears almost completely, and it becomes a propaganda agent for the Pentagon. As Dan Rather observed in his 1999 book *Deadlines and Datelines*, "The fact is, and the record shows, American journalists as a whole are, and have been over the years, decidedly promilitary. Foreign reporters and other international observers often accuse us of favoring our armed forces, and they're right. We try not to show our bias, but it manifests itself almost every time U.S. military forces are deployed anywhere in the world."

Even during peacetime, the military maintains close relations with the media. Dutch reporter Abe de Vries revealed that in 1999, CNN employed army propaganda experts from the Fourth Psychological Operations Group. Major Thomas Collins of the U.S. Army Information Service declared that the "psyops personnel" worked at CNN in Atlanta as "regular employees of CNN" as part of the army's "Training with Industry" program and "helped in the production of news."

Although reporters' patriotism is one reason that critical reporting disappears during a war, journalists have a genuine problem getting independent information when government secrecy is considered acceptable. During the Gulf War and other major conflicts, the Pentagon maintained strict censorship over reporters and provided the pictures it wants to show, to the point of deceiving journalists and the public about the accuracy of its bombing missions that killed thousands of civilians in Iraq. Indeed, most of the debates over wartime policy reflect internal Pentagon arguments, not the perspective of those who believe that war is unnecessary. When the bombs fall, the standards of journalism fall with them.

The Media on Bended Knee

In an age when politicians are celebrities (and sometimes vice versa) and competition among journalists is intense, news departments can't rely on having easy access to anyone. Politicians can threaten not to appear on Sunday morning talk shows if they might be asked challenging questions. When Newt Gingrich took over as Speaker, he boycotted the Sunday talk shows for a month because he didn't like the critical questions and refused for several weeks to answer questions from the *Atlanta Journal-Constitution*'s reporters because the paper printed a cartoon he didn't like. Gingrich even met behind closed doors with the CEOs of media conglomerates, complaining about critical reporting and telling them to keep their journalists in line.

Candidates and politicians commonly give special access and information to major media such as the *New York Times*. The leading media such as the *Wall Street Journal* receive (and often demand) exclusives on business mergers, and in exchange they promise not to quote anyone critical of the companies. If any of the media took an adversarial approach, they would be shut out by the newsmakers. In this way, the media depend as much on the political and business establishment for prestige and ratings as the politicians and corporations depend on them for free publicity. The result is not an adversarial relationship in which the truth is revealed but a symbiotic relationship in which both sides have a direct interest in avoiding views outside the mainstream.

The failure of the media to adequately investigate a Democratic president and question a Democratic administration may have seemed to conservatives to be evidence of a liberal bias—even though the Democrats weren't liberals and the media were even more subservient to Ronald Reagan, George Bush, Bob Dole, and Newt Gingrich, who never faced the kind of intensive surveillance experienced by Bill Clinton.

But a proestablishment bias—which the media certainly have—is not the same as a liberal bias, and it's a far cry from a leftist bias. Because of the conservative influence brought by campaign bribery and lobbying, the media's proestablishment bias tends to be a conservative bias—although the far right obviously doesn't see it that way when a Democrat is the president. The proestablishment bias, after all, sometimes excludes the far right voices, much to the annoyance of conservatives—who hardly care that progressive views are even more marginalized.

Most journalism bears no resemblance to aggressive investigative journalism. In fact, most media coverage bears no connection to journalism: it's entertainment, weather, features, sports, comics, and, most of all, advertising, with a small news hole. The main goal of most TV news departments is to produce cheap, ratings-driven features; most informational radio is devoted to the same news headlines repeated every ten minutes or to talk shows that tilt wildly to the right and are freed from any journalistic standards. Even newspapers devote surprisingly little space to actual news. It's simply not a priority: at the *Chicago Tribune*, one sports columnist is paid $225,000, twice as much as the maximum for any news editor. When infotainment reigns supreme over investigative journalism, the news will deviate little from the establishment's views.

The Media on Crack: Covering Up for the CIA

In August 1996, journalist Gary Webb of the *San Jose Mercury News* shook the world with a series of articles revealing links between the CIA's operations and drug dealing, including some of the major figures who helped launch the crack epidemic during the 1980s in California. If the media were liberal, or even neutral, the reaction should have been predictable: widespread praise, a Pulitzer Prize and other honors, and follow-up investigations on the ties between the U.S. government and all sorts of loathsome characters.

Instead, Webb faced a smear campaign from all the top newspapers, an attack unprecedented in the history of journalism. His colleagues seemed determined to undermine his articles, and when it proved impossible to refute fairly what he had written, they went after an absurd hyperbole of his journalism.

Webb's CIA/crack story is still probably the most widely read piece of journalism ever written. Webb, who for his series was named "Journalist of the Year" by the Northern California chapter of the Society of Professional Journalists, lost his job over this solid piece of investigative reporting, a clear example of how the media regulate journalists who dare examine an issue embarrassing to our government.

The evidence of the CIA's knowledge and tacit approval of drug dealing by its clients is overwhelming. That's why the CIA defenders ignored this fact and tried to claim that Webb was making a much stronger claim. CIA head John Deutch went to Los Angeles in order to refute "charges that the CIA introduced crack cocaine into South Central Los Angeles in the mid-1980s." Of course, Webb never claimed that they did. "The inquiry has not uncovered any evidence that Ricky Ross was used as a pawn to distribute cocaine to specific neighborhoods," declared a Los Angeles sheriff's department official about a key drug dealer after an investigation. Of course, this was never what Webb wrote. But a few conspiracy-minded individuals imagined that this was the case, prompting the mainstream press to "refute" the charge that the CIA secretly poured crack into Los Angeles as part of some secret plot to destroy the lives of African Americans—a charge that Webb never made.

The real issue of Webb's series was whether the CIA had tolerated Nicaraguan drug dealers supporting the *contras*. At the same time that the Reagan administration was pushing a war on drugs, Webb found, the CIA was protecting cocaine imports that helped spark the crack epidemic in Los Angeles.

No one imagines that the crack epidemic would have gone away without the CIA's assistance to a few "freedom-fighting" drug lords, but no one can deny the importance of these early drug imports. *Los Angeles Times* reporter Jesse Katz wrote one of the stories attacking Webb and contended that "how the crack epidemic reached that extreme, on some level, had nothing to do with Ross. Before and after his reign, a bewildering roster of other dealers and suppliers helped fuel the crisis. They were all responding to market forces that many experts believe would have created the problem whether any one individual sold crack or not." However, less than two years earlier, Katz himself had written in a December 20, 1994, story: "If there was an eye to the storm, if there was a criminal mastermind behind crack's decade-long reign, if there was one outlaw capitalist most responsible for flooding Los Angeles' streets with mass-marketed cocaine, his name was Freeway Rick."

Webb never attributed as much importance to Ricky Ross as Katz had in that 1994 story, but clearly Ross was responsible for tons of cocaine reaching addicts in the form of crack. Undoubtedly, the crack epidemic would have occurred without Ross, but he helped intensify the extent of it and the damage it wrought. If law enforcement officers had more time to respond to the crack epidemic and the crime wave it sparked in America, perhaps it would have been possible to organize a better response, but the failure in America to take effective action against drug epidemics is hardly Webb's fault.

The crux of Webb's story is that CIA officials knew about the drug dealing but kept it secret. Whether one endorses this covert policy depends on how one views the virtues of spurring civil war in Nicaragua and the spread of crack in America, but the accuracy of Webb's account is no longer in serious dispute.

Only the extent of the crack trade is debated. Roberto Suro

and Walter Pincus (who once worked for the CIA) wrote a *Washington Post* cover story entitled "CIA and Crack: Evidence Is Lacking of Contra-Tied Plot." Their principal contention was that Nicaraguan drug dealer Danilo Blandon "handled a total of only about five tons of cocaine during a decade-long career," although most people would consider 10,000 pounds of cocaine to be a considerable quantity.

The CIA's involvement in drugs went far beyond the Nicaraguan conflict, as Alexander Cockburn and Jeffrey St. Clair revealed in their book *Whiteout: The CIA, Drugs, and the Press.* Oliver North's notebooks even include a 1984 entry about a CIA man who wanted an aircraft to pick up 1,500 kilos of "paste" (cocaine paste) in Bolivia.

Webb's series revealed far more than the fact that the CIA was willing to overlook drug dealing in its relentless efforts to overthrow the Nicaraguan government. It exposed the mainstream media's role as apologists for the authorities. It was bad enough that major newspapers ignored the CIA-*contra*-crack link when the information was first uncovered in the 1980s by a congressional investigation. But to launch a crusade against the journalist who printed the important news they had overlooked amounted to sacrificing journalistic ethics for professional jealousy.

As Webb himself noted, "Nothing in their stories says there is anything wrong with what I wrote. In fact, they have confirmed every element of it." But the mainstream press spun the evidence indicating CIA involvement as if it were an exoneration, based on the strange idea that Webb had asserted some kind of CIA conspiracy attempted to push crack in certain neighborhoods.

The Webb case offers several lessons to progressives. First, it should eliminate any delusions about the willingness of the mainstream press to ignore stories that question powerful institutions. The more important and revealing a story is, the less likely it will ever appear in the establishment press. Progressives should also be aware of how dangerous it can be to associate with radical conspiracy theories. In the Webb case, journalists and government officials used the most extreme rumors to dismiss the most accurate reporting.

When the pressure from the mainstream media grew intense, *San Jose Mercury News* executive editor Jerry Ceppos buckled, apologizing for Webb's investigation. Webb's follow-up stories—proving that what he had written was accurate and expanding the investigation—weren't published. As retaliation, Webb was eventually exiled to the newspaper's Cupertino bureau, far away from his family and from any compelling stories to report. No longer allowed to be an investigative journalist, Webb resigned.

In the end, the title of Webb's series, "Dark Alliance," proved to be prescient. But rather than simply revealing a dark alliance between the CIA and pro-*contra* Nicaraguan drug dealers, his case showed a dark alliance between the media and the political establishment to conceal embarrassing evidence of misbehavior by government officials that helped spread the devastating epidemic of drugs in America.

Conclusion: The Reign of the Conservative Media

Why do Americans perceive a liberal media? One reason is the mythology of the media: we still imagine journalists to be like Bob Woodward and Carl Bernstein, who aggressively pursued President Nixon's crimes and forced him out of office. The fact that so few journalists (not even Woodward and Bernstein) act that way anymore, or ever did, doesn't stop the myth from persisting.

Another reason that people perceive the media as liberal is that the public tends to notice only unusual reporting. There is a conservative baseline for the media that the public has taken as the norm: when the media follow the status quo, nobody sees it. But if the media on rare occasions actually investigate the political establishment, it sticks in people's minds. So they perceive the media as liberal, perhaps because the public sees the even greater conservative control over the political mainstream.

According to conservatives, corporate America is the victim of a devious liberal media conspiracy. Big media corporations hire liberal reporters who attack them. Big corporations advertise in these proliberal newspapers. Wealthy, conservative people subscribe to these proliberal newspapers. Yet the well-paid "liberal" journalists, like the lovable prisoners in *Hogan's Heroes* who run a spy operation under Colonel Klink's monocled eye, secretly evade their profit-hungry bosses, their advertisers, and their readers in order to spread the message of the left through various secret codes cleverly inserted into those stories passively quoting government officials and business executives.

The conservative conspiracy theories don't make any sense. Millionaire TV anchors twisting the news in favor of the poor? Corporate executives applauding the journalists who attack the companies they run? Liberal bias isn't a profitable endeavor. It goes against every rule of capitalism and journalism for liberal bias to dominate the media. In a free market, a liberal media bias could never survive. And it hasn't.

Why, then, do the charges of liberal bias stick? Because Rush Limbaugh and a legion of right-wing talk show hosts and opinion writers regularly repeat that the media are liberal, and the absence of progressive voices in the mainstream media makes it difficult for the opposing view to be heard. For the media owners, allegations of a liberal bias make it easier for them to impose the conservative bias they prefer. For the pseudoliberals who work in the media system, confessing to a liberal bias is far more comfortable than admitting that they've sold out their beliefs for a nice salary. It's only because the mainstream media is so conservative that all these right-wing pundits can make accusations of liberal bias without opposition.

Progressives do, however, bear some responsibility for the perception that the media are liberal. Although a few organizations point out the media's conservative bias (most notably Fairness and Accuracy In Reporting) and a few progressive magazines haphazardly discuss it, many leftists would rather march in a protest than write a letter to the editor.

One mistake many progressives make is to try to defend the media against conservative attacks. Staying on the defensive only makes it seem like the media really are liberal. While it's important to refute inaccurate conservative allegations of liberal bias, the best way to do that is by going on the offensive and pointing out the procorporate, right-wing bias at every opportunity.

Progressives can change the conservative bias of the media and challenge the media biases at every turn. Letters to the editor, calls to radio talk shows, participation in media watch organizations—all these tactics are important to counter the public's misperception of a liberal media and to present a progressive perspective on various issues. Equally important is the creation of alternative media—newspapers, magazines, web sites, radio programs, cable access programs—that provide a place for stories and perspectives excluded from the mainstream media.

By demanding an equal place in the media, progressives can swing the political debate in their direction. In a political system corrupted by money, progressives will always be at a disadvantage. But if progressive ideas can be heard in the media, the left will have an advantage in shaping the future of American politics.

Chapter 7

THE GLOBALIZATION WARS

How the Left Won (and Lost) the "Battle in Seattle"

Victory isn't easy for the left, even when it wins. One example in which progressives did almost everything right (but nevertheless was widely attacked) was the 1999 World Trade Organization (WTO) hearings in Seattle. Thanks to the hard work of leftists around the country (and the world), Seattle was overrun by more than 50,000 protesters who were determined to bring public attention to a powerful, secretive trade group.

A huge rally organized by labor groups brought tens of thousands marching through Seattle, complete with union workers and environmentalists in sea turtle costumes. Thousands of protesters linked arms and prevented the opening session of the WTO from meeting.

Most of the media coverage blamed the protesters for property damage that was planned and caused by anarchists and not stopped by the police.

But the protesters did have a powerful effect on the scene, where the bias of the American media was less important to the delegates, many of whom sympathized with some of the protests. President Clinton, the world's leading trend detector, expressed his support for listening to the peaceful protesters, showing that he was more alert to the persuasive power of the anti-WTO forces than most of the media.

Seattle and Washington left the left with many lessons. The first was never to let the media choose what the issue would be. Unfortunately, journalists (and their editors) are trained to overlook an important point for the sake of a flashy image and to portray a dramatic confrontation rather than a moral cause. This doesn't excuse the inaccurate reporting, biased attacks, and unquestioning defense of the authorities that filled most of the front pages and TV news about the WTO and IMF demonstrations. The progressives failed to spin the issue beyond their simple anti-WTO message. The reasons for opposing the WTO got some mention, but the idea of an alternative international organization built on genuine "free trade" and the protection of basic human rights never was aired.

The left has become so accustomed to being ignored that progressives have wisely refined the attention-grabbing techniques of theatrical protest that can convey a simple message. Unfortunately, the left hasn't developed the difficult techniques of bringing more complex arguments into the public debate, and the result is that progressive views seem shallow and emotional compared with the more extensive coverage of the ideas of the right and the center in the mainstream media.

Still, Seattle was both a success and an opportunity lost. The left brought attention to an organization without many redeeming values, but it never was able to launch a serious debate about what the alternative global values should be.

Ignoring the massive evidence of police misconduct and

y, the media served a well-defined role as gatekeepers uth. When the media criticized Seattle officials, it was for "permitting" the peaceful protestors to exercise their right to protest instead of shutting down the city, as happened for the rest of the WTO meetings.

Still, the inability of the left to unify their ideas as easily as they unified behind the physical protest made it possible for many of the media errors to go unchallenged. Imagine if all the groups united behind the WTO protests had planned to meet after the initial melee and formulate a united response. Imagine if they had declared,

> We denounce all violence, whether it is the violence of smashing windows; the violence of shooting tear gas, concussion grenades, pepper spray, and rubber bullets at peaceful protestors; or the violence of regimes anywhere in the world where political, human, or labor rights are violated and the environment is harmed.

> We regret that the police chose to ignore the vandalism on the streets of downtown Seattle and instead attacked nonviolent protestors with tear gas and rubber bullets. As we informed police before the protests began, a group of violent anarchists had announced their intention to try to disrupt our nonviolent protests and discredit our cause. Although many peaceful demonstrators defended Seattle's stores—some of which we had previously protested in front of—against property damage and looting, we could not persuade these well-organized anarchists to stop, and we could not persuade the police shooting tear gas at us to stop the violence.

> We remain united in our belief that the policies of the World Trade Organization are harmful to the people of the world and are designed instead to increase the profits of corporations and the politicians who serve them. We will return to down-

town Seattle to exercise our constitutional rights to assemble peacefully and express our ideas about the WTO.

Saying that the WTO should be abolished is a simple and perhaps desirable goal. But failing to present a comprehensive alternative to international trade left the protesters open to accusations of being naive or protectionist. The problem for the left was that their efforts were so disorganized that no clear alternative emerged. There was no comprehensive solution offered for the problems posed by the WTO, the World Bank, and the IMF. No alternative institutions were proposed to take over the work of helping the world rather than harming it.

Progressives need an international approach to free trade that doesn't seem like protectionism. "America First" is not a progressive perspective, and it fails to help the rest of the world. Without a progressive vision of globalism, the protests against free trade begin to merge with narrow-minded Buchananesque conspiracy theories about the UN or the WTO taking over the world.

The "Free Trade" Debate

"We demand fair trade, not free trade," declared the protestors against the World Trade Organization's 1999 meeting in Seattle. Fair is a fine word, but so is free. When progressives allow themselves to be defined, as opposed to free trade, it becomes difficult to win an argument—especially among the American intelligentsia, to whom the bias against "fair trade" is overwhelming.

There is no position held more fervently by the American elite than free trade. Democrats, Republicans, and media professionals all share a belief in "free trade," even if they rarely understand what it means. It is virtually impossible to find

stream politician or pundit willing to criticize "free
ven though the majority of the American people are
tar more skeptical of it.

FREE TRADE AND ECONOMIC LIBERTY

All trade agreements are efforts to force nations to adopt policies that they otherwise would oppose. But "free trade" agreements only try to impose certain economic rules, such as limits on tariffs or promises to enforce antipirating laws. Why should it be more important to force China to respect intellectual property rights instead of human rights? Why should second-rate movies have more rights than human beings? From an economic point of view, political repression restricts people in their freedom to work at least as much as do restrictions on "free trade." If a country must promise not to take away property rights by seizing businesses in order to join the international economic community, why shouldn't a country be forced to promise not to take away human rights by seizing protesters?

Conservatives like to argue that free trade is good because economic liberty leads to political liberty. Progressives need to realize that the right is right on this basic principle. Economic liberty is essential to both democracy and political freedom.

That doesn't mean that reduced tariffs will inevitably lead to open elections in China and the rest of the world. The blind spot of conservatives is their narrow, inadequate definition of "economic liberty." The right defines economic freedom under "free trade" as merely the freedom to sell goods to other countries, the removal of special subsidies to domestic industries, and the enforcement of certain property rights. Yet economic freedom, properly understood, must incorporate many other rights: the right to form a union; the right of children not to be forced to work; the right to receive overtime and holidays; the right to safe and healthy working conditions.

> Conservatives also fail to understand how the basic principles of free trade must logically include international work standards. From an economic point of view, there is no difference among a tariff protecting an industry, a direct subsidy to a particular industry, and weak environmental or safety regulations that are worth the equivalent amount to an industry. Therefore, if "free trade" demands the removal of corporate subsidies—as it absolutely should—then all these impediments to free trade should be fought equally.

I've always had a troubled relationship with the antitrade segment of the left. I am an advocate of "free trade" at heart, and so I split from the left on this particular issue. Or at least that's what I thought. I thought the opposition to "free trade" (a phrase I've never put in quotation marks until now) was simply a reactionary, Pat Buchanan–style desire to put a Great Wall around America and let nothing in.

What changed my mind? How does a free trader cross the border to become a fair trader? First of all, the "free trade" versus "fair trade" dichotomy didn't help. Ask me to choose between "free" and "fair" trade, and I'll vacillate for a while. Both "free" and "fair" are powerful, ill-defined concepts.

Of course, it is important to work toward both "fair trade" and "free trade"—making sure that foreign companies manufacturing products for multinational corporations will pay a living wage, not use child labor, not destroy the environment, and protect the right to unionize.

International trade organizations do have the potential to serve progressive goals. In February 2000, the WTO actually ruled for the European Union against the United States over a hidden $3.5 billion annual subsidy given by the U.S. government to large corporations. The United States allows American companies to set up front corporations for exports in tax havens, which allows these companies to give a part of their export profits to these subsidiaries tax free. The expense of setting up these shell companies prevents smaller exporters from getting the tax breaks. Corporate welfare on this scale is one reason that individuals must pay higher and higher taxes to make up for all the tax breaks given away to big American companies.

If U.S. citizens tried to reduce their tax bill by claiming that some of their income shouldn't be taxed, they'd be thrown in prison for tax evasion. But when influential companies are the beneficiaries, Congress passes laws to defend the corporate welfare, and U.S. trade officials rush to support it.

The export tax break is precisely the kind of issue that progressives need to raise in order to gain credibility on the trade debate. These illicit corporate welfare programs show that it's the big corporations that oppose genuine free trade. By attacking the export tax break and similar corporate subsidies, progressives can prove that they're not against trade. They can also counter the myth that the United States is a paragon of free trade.

In fact, no government in the world subsidizes its businesses as much as the United States does. From direct subsidies to corporate farmers (the $21 billion paid out in 1999 must have exceeded the payments by any other country, not to mention the subsidized grazing charges on public lands used to help corporate ranchers) to the subsidized wasteful use of natural resources (through funding private transit rather than public transit, by keeping the gasoline tax far below the social costs of transit, and by providing resources such as minerals and trees on public land to private companies at prices far below the market rate), the United States is the king of corporate welfare. America's bloated defense budget provides huge amounts of money to corporations with virtually no oversight.

Because U.S. officials always present themselves as the defenders of free trade and attack foreign restrictions and subsidies on behalf of American companies, everyone imagines that the United States is somehow devoted to free trade. Yet if America truly represented the pinnacle of free trade, why would it be "unfree" trade to require countries to recognize the right to form labor unions, environmental regulations, antidiscrimination laws, a minimum wage, and similar U.S. policies? If there's free trade in America despite all these factors, how could these policies make trade "unfree" in the rest of the world?

It's dangerous for progressives to be slapped with the label of opposing free trade. That's why it's important for the left to offer a program to increase "free trade" while simultaneously protecting environmental and labor laws. While some progressives have gotten hooked on the slogan of "fair trade, not free trade," the truth is that if it's properly understood, "free trade" ought to be a progressive position. When progressives seek only to oppose "free trade" rather than question its meaning, they've already lost the argument in the minds of many people.

We must interact more with the rest of the planet, but there are many different ways to globalize: some of them help people, and some of them help corporations. Will we choose globalization that protects environmental, labor, and human rights? Or globalization that undermines these rights? The WTO has never expanded environmental, labor, or human rights regulations, while in its short life the organization has ruled against national laws that protect these rights. The ideal is not for national laws to trump all international agreements but for international laws and treaties to protect important regulations as well as freedom of trade.

By adopting a position in favor of free and fair trade, progressives can overcome the traditional association of free trade critics with narrow-minded protectionism. Criticizing the WTO and leading sea turtles down the streets of Seattle are only the opening salvo of a fight in which the left must offer alternative ways to build international institutions to ensure both free and fair trade. Refusing to choose between these words must be the first step in a rhetorical strategy to convince the world.

The procorporate definition of "free trade" must not be accepted without a fight. Trade based on child labor is not "free." Trade based on denying the right to unionize is not "free." Trade based on endangering workers is not "free." Trade based on forced prison labor is not "free." Trade based on polluting the environment is not "free." Human beings subsidize this "free" trade with the lost potential of our children, with maimed and killed workers, with human rights sacrificed, and with the damage to the environment that endangers our lives and that governments today and in the future must pay to clean up.

Genuine free trade would prohibit sweatshops, prohibit abuses of human and labor rights, and prevent the massive pollution of the environment. Even if this is not entirely possible through trade agreements, at the very least an international trade organization must encourage these changes just as much as it encourages the end of protectionism. Considering that the WTO frequently ruled against these measures, the organization was worse than useless and moved the world away from genuine economic freedom.

STOPPING SWEATSHOPS ON COLLEGE CAMPUSES

It's remarkable to imagine that a group of college students could help change working conditions at factories around the world. Yet that's what happened when students protested the fact that apparel with their university's name on it could be made using sweatshop labor at Third World factories. No one could accuse the students of simply being self-interested or joining a protest because it's the trendy thing to do. Protesting against sweatshops was an entirely selfless cause.

The pressure was powerful enough that the sweatshop profiteers, with the help of university administrators, created an industry front group, the Fair Labor Association, supposedly to prevent these abuses. Even this was a small, but real, accomplishment. A bunch of liberals would have been satisfied, but these students weren't. They started pressuring their colleges to reject the industry-supported group and instead endorse an alternative, independent certification organization, the Worker Rights Coalition.

After giving the administrators several months to act, the protestors took over the president's office at colleges around the country, from the University of Pennsylvania to the University of Wisconsin (where they were forcibly removed by police and arrested) to the University of Michigan. To most administrators, opposing help for underpaid and abused workers halfway around the world didn't sound like a sensible position.

The new generation of student protestors is smarter and more effective than their more radical campus ancestors. These college students created the perfect combination of local work for a larger cause. They were well organized, with a coalition of international antisweatshop groups helping support their efforts.

The goal behind the General Agreement on Tariffs and Trade (GATT) and the World Trade Organization all too often is not "free trade" benefiting everyone but probusiness trade aimed at increasing corporate profits. That's why corporations and the governments they influence are opposed to genuine free trade that protects environmental and labor rights.

The alternative of protectionism cannot be a progressive position. Protecting American jobs by preventing foreign workers from obtaining jobs is a nationalist not a progressive ideal.

Protectionism costs consumers huge amounts of money, pumps up corporate profits, and ultimately fails to prevent American jobs from moving overseas. The only way to protect American jobs from unfair competition is to ensure that proper labor and human rights standards are followed around the world and also in the United States.

If progressives simply try to fight against free trade, they will be on the losing side of history. But if progressives fight for genuine free trade, they will have an opportunity to seize the terms of the debate from corporate interests. Progressives need to realize that free trade is a wonderful goal. The only question is whether it will be a limited "free trade" to protect the freedom of corporations to make money or a true free trade that defends the freedom of workers and citizens to protect their rights and their planet.

Chapter 8

PRAGMATIC PROGRESSIVES

Progressives need to be pragmatic in order to be powerful. However, pragmatism shouldn't be confused with Clintonian centrism and the abandonment of all substance. Pragmatists have principles, too. The difference between a pragmatic progressive and a foolish one is the willingness to pick the right fights and fight in the right way to accomplish these same goals.

The current failure of progressivism in America is due to the structure of American politics and media, not because of a wrong turn that the movement took somewhere along the way. What the left needs is not a "better" ideology but a tactical adaptation to the obstacles it faces in the contemporary political scene. A pragmatic progressivism does not sacrifice its ideals but simply communicates them better to the larger public.

The words we use shape how people respond to our ideas. It's tempting to offer the standard advice that progressives should present their ideas in the most palatable form. But palatable to whom? The media managers and pedestrian pundits who are the intellectual gatekeepers won't accept these ideas. By the time progressives transform their ideas into the political baby food necessary for inclusion in current debates, it barely seems to be worth the effort.

Leftists need to seize the dominant political rhetoric, even though it may be conservative in its goals, and turn it in a progressive direction. Progressives need to use the antitax ideology to demand tax cuts for the poor. Progressives need to use the antigovernment and antiwelfare ideology to demand the end of corporate welfare. Progressives need to translate every important issue into the language that is permissible in the mainstream. Something will inevitably be lost in the translation. But the political soul underlying these progressive ideas can be preserved and brought to the public's attention.

The left does not need to abandon its progressive views in order to be popular. The left only needs to abandon some of its failed strategies and become as savvy as the conservatives are at manipulating the press and the politicians. The language of progressives needs to become more mainstream, but the ideas must remain radical. In an age of soulless politicians and spineless ideologies, the left has the virtue of integrity. Until progressives become less self-satisfied with the knowledge that they're right and more determined to convince everyone else of this fact, opportunities for political change will not be forthcoming.

Progressives have also been hampered by a revolutionary instinct among some leftist groups. According to some left wingers, incremental progress is worthless—that is, nothing short of a radical change in government will mean anything to them. Indeed, for the most radical left wingers, liberal reforms are a threat to the movement, since they reduce the desire for more extreme changes.

What the revolutionaries fail to realize is that progressive achievements can build on one another. If anything approaching a political revolution actually happens in America, it will be due to a succession of popular, effective, progressive reforms. A popular uprising in the ballot box is possible only if the left can change its political assumptions about smaller, specific issues.

Revolution versus Reform

The left often finds itself stuck in a debate between revolution and reform. To self-described revolutionaries, any attempt to reform the system is a liberal compromise that only delays the creation of a socialist utopia.

The vision of workers casting off their chains and embracing the overthrow of capitalism is pure fantasy. No one actually knows what it means to overthrow capitalism, and it clearly isn't going to happen, anyway.

Reforming American capitalism is not a halfhearted effort at modest change; it is a fundamental attack on the reigning ideology of "free market" capitalism. Progressive reforms, taken seriously, are revolutionary in every important sense.

Reforms such as the New Deal were truly revolutionary for their time, and American capitalism has been saved from its own flaws by these progressive reforms. The problem is that these progressive reforms have not been carried far enough, in part because the revolutionary left has too often failed to support the progressives' reformist agenda. The only leftist revolution in America will come from an accumulation of progressive policies, and so the question of revolution versus reform is irrelevant.

The Diverse Left

Many philosophers of the left propose solving all the problems posed to progressives by uniting the left behind some single universal principle of class, abandoning its diverse obsessions with race, gender, sexual orientation, environmentalism, and all the other "isms" of the left.

A left that works for the working class is not incompatible, however, with a left that campaigns for equality on the basis of race, gender, sexual orientation, disability, age, and so on. If progressives ignore the fact that African Americans or women or gays and lesbians face inequality and discrimination, no one will take them seriously when they argue that the poor are treated unjustly. A theory of oppression that challenges the American presumption of equality must encompass all these oppressions, not just the ones that seem most politically palatable.

Conservative forces developed the term *special-interest groups* to attack progressive causes. For Republicans, it became the way to attack the best-organized leftist parts of the Democratic Party. For Democrats, denouncing "special interests" has been the favorite tactic of centrist candidates who want to eliminate progressive forces with their own party. The special-interest groups are not nearly as special as the corporate interests. The "special interests" have relatively little power, even within the Democratic Party, and they represent a far larger part of America than do the corporations that often oppose them.

Progressives are tagged with the label of being the servants of "special interests"—blacks, Latinos, women, gays and lesbians, labor unions, the poor, the disabled, and so forth. Of course, if you add up all the "special interests" supposedly beholden to the left, they represent more than 90 percent of the population. Obviously, it's the right and the neoliberals who serve the truly "special" interests: rich straight white men and the corporations they run.

There is no inherent conflict between the so-called special interests on the left and the ideal of common progressive ideals. The goal of liberty and equality requires addressing the injustices affecting these so-called special interests. No progressive movement can be true to its name unless it speaks out against racial discrimination, gender inequality, homophobia, and any other forms of oppression. Progressives must demand that class be added to these issues, but class analysis alone cannot adequately address all inequalities. Class alone does not explain why the wealthy African American driving a BMW gets pulled over by the police. Class alone does not explain why women face a glass ceiling (or, even more often, a glass door). Exclusively class-based solutions may help some poor white males who legitimately need assistance, but class ignores too many other important factors.

It's the unequal treatment of women and minorities that helps create many of these class inequities, and the politics of racism and sexism that prevents the public from looking at the inequities created by class. Both the Republican and Democratic Parties are notorious for using race to distract poor whites from the poverty they face and to prevent them from organizing to achieve greater equality. The answer to this problem is not to abandon the cause of racial equality in hopes of building a larger progressive movement based on appealing to racists. The left can succeed only if it has principles. What the left needs to do is communicate the fact that these principles promote an ideal of equality that includes advancing the cause of poor people of all races.

Race and gender analysis does not distract us from understanding an overarching principle of class. On the contrary, no one can understand how class inequalities exist in America without comprehending how racial bias and gender discrimination create many of these class inequities. Class is not a magical word capable of bringing the masses to progressive causes, any more than race or gender has brought success to the left. Progressives need to cast a wide net of interlinked causes that can be pursued separately while still contributing to the ultimate goal of justice and equality.

The left needs intellectuals and activists, academics and anarchists, special-interest groups and broad coalitions, Marxist ideologies and crazed hippies, atheists and religious freaks, reformers and revolutionaries, and everybody else. This is the left. It cannot be controlled, but it can be nudged. The diverse left cannot be led down a single path, but perhaps it can be guided in a general direction. Or at the very least, perhaps the left can be persuaded to give up its internal bickering and recognize its common foes.

RIGHT-WING NUTS AND OTHER EXTREMISTS

It sometimes can be tempting for progressives to dismiss the opposition as a bunch of extremist nuts, cranks, and assorted crackpots, whose lunacy is matched only by their stupidity. It can be especially tempting because the far right also views most progressives as the "loony left."

Extremism in the attack on extremism is ineffective. It may be difficult to convert a hard-core conservative, but engaging in sound, well-reasoned arguments with the far right can be an effective way of converting many people in the middle. Making progressive policies look acceptable to the mainstream is made harder, not easier, by engaging in a war of hyperbole with the far right.

There are times when it's appropriate to call a nut a nut. Because so many of the mainstream media accept far right ideas as perfectly acceptable, honesty can sometimes help, by condemning a thoroughly evil idea as "completely wacko." Most of the time, though, it's more effective for progressives to be the voice of reason, not the voice of judgment.

Usually it's best to let the far right hang themselves with their conspiracy theories and misguided schemes. Most people sympathize with and support someone who seems closer to their ideas or at least someone who is willing to try to understand their point of view. It's also helpful to find points of agreement with the "right-wing nuts"—after all, if the far right is willing to support a few progressive ideas, it might be possible to make a coalition on certain issues. Many "right-wing nuts" aren't nuts about everything: some libertarians attack corporate welfare, some religious conservatives oppose the death penalty, and some populists oppose unfair—and unfree—trade policies. Some "right-wing nuts" might be converted to progressive causes if they ever heard a persuasive proponent.

The goal of avoiding nasty insults shouldn't be confused with a kinder, gentler rhetoric. There's plenty of room for passionate arguments and a strong condemnation of political corruption without dismissing as a "right-wing nut" anyone who disagrees with you.

Pundits often attribute the rise of conservatism to its adherents' willingness to put aside internal differences and unite for a single cause. They're dead wrong. The Republican Party today is a collage of contradictory forces: the corporate welfare capitalists, the libertarian fringe, the religious right, and many more.

To be sure, the most powerful and conservative elements of the Republican Party control its more moderate elements. A hint that a presidential candidate is prochoice in any way, for example, promotes an immediate backlash. But within the far right, an enormous diversity of ideas is tolerated in the pursuit of power.

Many pundits on the left preach unity by dissolving all the "special interest" groups. The left's diversity is its strongest attribute, however; consider that the Democratic Party, despite having enormous resources, millions of voters, and a pipeline to power, has relatively few active volunteers compared with those in the numerous leftist groups working tirelessly to achieve their goals. If the Democratic Party were willing to pursue progressive policies, it might lose some of its money, but it would gain many more human activists.

The Leftist Underdog

Because of the power of media corporations and political money, progressives must constantly fight an uphill battle just to be heard. Progressives are like a political candidate facing an incumbent who has all the money, all the endorsements, and all the connections. For that reason, progressives must rely on free media to get their message out. That's why the left often relies on protests, parades, and performance political art—because the media usually won't cover their press conferences or invite them to appear on talk shows.

The position of being the permanent political underdog isn't easy. Unlike the movies, in real life the underdog usually loses, often without putting up much of a fight. What progressives need to do is understand the role of the underdog without succumbing to feelings of hopelessness.

If the left can adopt strategies designed to win as the underdog, it can overcome some of the power of the establishment: their money, their political control, and their media dominance. No one expects progressivism to sweep across America. But it is possible to break through the media blackout on progressive ideas by adapting to American conservative rhetoric. Instead of only fighting right-wing notions of tax cuts, smaller government, and a war on welfare, leftists need to manipulate this rhetoric to draw attention to progressive causes. Instead of despairing over the hopelessness of getting progressive reforms enacted, leftists need to find ways to accomplish their aims.

The progressive role as the underdog also requires taking solace in small victories. Nobody in the American political system gets his or her way entirely; everyone must make compromises and accept partial solutions. Not even the far right, with its powerful hold over American politics in the 1980s, ever succeeded in having its agenda widely enacted. Progressives need to hold onto their values while they recognize that compromises will inevitably fall short of their ultimate goals.

Legislative compromises, however, don't mean that progressives must turn to centrism. Instead, the best hope for pragmatic progressives is to maintain their integrity. By creating a popular agenda and winning back control of the Democratic Party, progressives have the potential to take power away from the corporate interests that run American politics.

How Progressives Differ from Conservatives

Progressives often make the mistake of imagining that merely imitating conservative political tactics will bring leftists the same degree of influence that the far right now has over American politics. Progressives and conservatives could not be more different in their tactical positions. Conservatives have power but not popularity—the public hates their ideas, but their well-financed influence over the media and politics more than compensates for this failing. As a result, conservatives must constantly engage in a campaign of deceit by disguising what they believe in order to avoid alienating the American people.

Progressives have popularity but not power—the public would like their ideas if the left could ever have them taken seriously by the political and media powers-that-be. As a result, progressives must not imitate conservative tactics of deception. The notion that success in American politics requires moving rhetorically to the center in order to conceal one's true ideas is a tactic that applies only to the conservatives, who have manipulated the political process because they have no other choice.

Progressives don't need to lie; they need to overcome their power deficit. For this task, truth is the left's powerful ally. Progressives need to change their policy proposals not because they're unpopular but because a new approach is needed to break through the mainstream ban on progressive ideas. By bringing their popular values to the public, progressives can make dramatic changes in American politics.

Chapter 9

TALKING TAX CUTS

Lowering Taxes on the Poor

One of the problems that progressives face is the perception that everyone on the left wants to raise taxes. There's a partial truth here: the left certainly does want to shift much of the tax burden from the poor and working classes to the rich. But the overall perception that progressives want to tax and spend more money than conservatives do isn't necessarily true. In fact, if you look at the ideal budgets proposed by progressives, centrist Democrats like Bill Clinton, moderate Republicans, and the far right, it's the progressives who have the smallest government in mind.

The truth is that once you consider sharp defense cuts and greatly reduced corporate welfare (which together constitute a large part of the total government budget), the ideal budget proposed by most progressives is smaller than the current one, even when you add substantial increases in education, medical care, and social programs. The conservative vision of "small" government is small only with respect to its protections for the environment and political rights. When it comes to putting people in prison, giving handouts to big corporations, and inflating the defense budget beyond any possible military necessity, the right is the party of big government.

Why, then, are conservatives perceived as the advocates of small government while liberals are perceived as wasteful spenders? One reason is that conservatives have a powerful influence over the Republican Party, whereas progressives have almost no power over the Democratic Party. The "left-of-center" Clinton Democrats in control support corporate welfare and defense spending, since the beneficiaries of this government largesse provide a major source of campaign contributions for them. The Democratic Party maintains its liberal credentials by supporting somewhat higher social spending than the Republicans do. As a result, the Democrats usually are the party of big government, but there's no reason that the progressive movement in America should be stuck with the same label.

Nonetheless, the myth of progressives favoring big government persists. In part, the myth is spread by the right, which opposes progressive "big government" regulations that improve working conditions and protect the environment. Health and safety regulations are only a tiny part of the government's budget (made even smaller with the rise of the far right's influence on American politics). The "cost" is imposed on businesses that must spend more money when they would prefer to pollute the environment or harm workers without any financial consequences.

The left itself promotes the "tax-and-spend" myth. In an era when "read my lips—no new taxes" became the prevailing ideology, calling oneself a "tax-and-spend" Democrat—as erstwhile candidate Warren Beatty did in one speech—is a badge of courage. But is a progressive like Beatty really in favor of higher taxes and more government spending? Would his ideal budget—minus all the corporate welfare and wasteful programs—really be larger than today's government budget? "Tax-and-spend" is simply a misguided label meant to communicate a commitment to social programs but ultimately fails to promote progressive ideas.

What's so bad about big government? Nothing. Most people would not be opposed to living under a European system with a much larger percentage of its gross domestic product (GDP) devoted to taxes and government spending. In fact, the idea that "big government" is destroying America is simply nonsense. As a proportion of GDP, the U.S. government is now smaller than it was in 1964, before President Lyndon Johnson created his Great Society programs. After hitting a peak during the defense-fueled deficits of the Reagan presidency, the size of the federal government has steadily decreased as a percentage of GDP.

Anyone suggesting a "big government" approach in America is fighting an uphill battle against a long antitax tradition. Since America is wealthy enough to sustain adequate social spending on a relatively small proportion of GDP, progressives don't need to make a complicated case for bigger government. Rather, what the left must do is change the budget priorities that give ridiculous amounts of funding to corporate interests. Income taxes have remained steady for more than a half century at about 50 percent of federal government revenues. The problem is that the proportion of revenue from excise taxes and corporate taxes has been cut in half during this period while payroll taxes have grown to fill the gap. If corporations paid their fair share, there could be huge tax breaks.

FAVORING THE FLAT TAX

The easiest way to argue against the flat tax is to endorse it. It's inconceivable, progressives may think, to support Steve Forbes's dumb plan (and it certainly is a dumb plan unless you're a millionaire) to cut taxes on rich people like himself. But instead of rejecting the flat tax out of hand, what if progressives demanded a flat tax that served the interests of the people? A progressive flat tax isn't an oxymoron—it's a way for the left to take the issue of tax reform away from conservatives.

Two factors determine how progressive an income tax system would be: the rate of taxation at different incomes, and the standard deduction. Progressives are accustomed to seeking a more progressive tax rate, rising as income increases. But there's no reason that the same result couldn't be achieved with a flat tax rate and a dramatically higher standard deduction.

The Forbes flat tax is an appalling giveaway to the wealthy that would add to the tax burden on the poor and the middle class. But imagine a progressive flat tax with a standard deduction of $20,000 for each individual (instead of the current $4,300 for singles and $7,200 for couples). After that, all income would be taxed at a rate of about 44 percent. A married couple with children could earn up to $50,000 tax free. The result would be lower taxes for 98 percent of Americans, a 100 percent tax break for the working poor, and a clear-cut, popular issue for progressives to stand on.

At the very least, a proposal to use any budget surplus tax cuts to raise the standard deduction (saving virtually every taxpayer, rich and poor alike, an equal $150 per $1,000 increase) would be a step in the right direction and a highly popular—but completely fair—tax cut. Whenever the right demands a flat tax, they can be asked whether they support the Forbes flat tax for the rich or the fair flat tax that helps everyone.

In all the discussions about lowering taxes, the poor get left out. The centrist Democrats care about giving tax credits to the middle class, since they're deemed to be the swing voters. The Republicans (and the Democrats) care about giving huge tax breaks to the wealthy, since they're the donors. And progressives have become so attached to fighting these tax cut proposals for the wealthy that they haven't proposed a popular alternative: substantially reducing taxes on the poor. Politically, it's an amazing opportunity: a substantial cut in taxes for all Americans living in poverty would require only a tiny tax increase on less than 1 percent of the richest people. But there is no political organization speaking up for this segment of society on tax issues.

The enormous inequality of wealth in America creates an easy chance for progressives to propose sharp tax cuts for the poor. Because the poor make so little money compared with the rich in America, their total federal income taxes are barely noticeable. The top 50 percent of wage earners pay 95.7 percent of federal income taxes (the top 25 percent pay 81 percent of the income taxes). This means that the government could essentially eliminate federal income taxes on anyone earning below the average income (around $25,000 a year) and lose only 4.3 percent of revenue—an amount that could be taken from the proposed budget surpluses or raised by a tiny increase on the taxes of the wealthiest 1 percent. A plan to eliminate income taxes on anyone earning less than $25,000 a year would be incredibly popular—and yet the dominant political debate is over how much money to give away to the rich.

No one familiar with American politics can underestimate the popularity of tax cuts. That's why the left has to adopt a new framework, shifting some of its priorities to adopt tax cuts for the poor. Instead of simply opposing conservative tax cuts for the rich, progressives need to offer some of their own—for the poor and the middle class.

One of the Clinton administration's most brilliant strategic moves was to increase funding for college students via a tax credit rather than increased spending on financial aid. The net effect of the two is roughly identical: helping middle-income families afford college. But the "tax cut" version—despite the added complexity in calculating one's taxes and the skewed benefit toward wealthier families—is far more politically palatable than the "increased spending" version.

Big corporations have known for a long time that new tax cuts are easier for Congress to pass than new programs are. That's why most corporate lobbyists in Washington now focus on tax cuts for their special interests rather than on direct spending on them. Now it's time for the advocates of poor people to do the same.

Progressives have fallen into the trap of believing the Republican attacks on liberal ideas. Because the right wingers accuse us of promoting big government, progressives show how progressive they are by defending big government programs. Changing the terms of the debate would benefit progressives far more: to make Republicans defend their wasteful programs and to push progressive tax cuts.

Instead of trying to create more social programs to help poor people who don't have enough money, why doesn't the left support efforts to cut taxes on working people? Sales taxes, property taxes, Social Security taxes, and state and federal income taxes all impose a heavy burden on the working poor.

Currently, we have a crazy tax system in which we heavily tax the working poor for Social Security and impose an income tax on them, but then we give them back some of the money with the earned-income tax credit (EITC). The EITC has drawn the ire of conservatives as a wasteful government program—but it could not be stopped because of the popularity of rewarding the working poor. Spending on the EITC grew from $6 billion in

1994 to $51 billion in 1999. Imagine if we simplified the system: reduced the payroll and income taxes on the working poor (while still giving them credit for Social Security) and eliminated much of the need for an earned-income tax credit.

RAISING THE MINIMUM WAGE

Ever since the first national minimum wage was created in 1938 (at 25 cents an hour), conservatives have attacked the idea of government "interference" in the economy. The minimum wage peaked at $7.50 an hour (in current dollars) in the late 1960s, far above even the current proposals for a future increase. If the minimum wage had grown with the rate of economic productivity or stock prices in America over the past thirty years, it would now be well over $10 an hour.

Conservatives assume that a higher minimum wage would hurt profits and jobs and that a low minimum wage is a cost-free approach. But that's not true. Government (and that means all of us as taxpayers) pays billions of dollars every year to subsidize this social policy of a low minimum wage. Because the minimum wage is so low, we spend huge amounts for the earned-income tax credit. The government gives up enormous tax revenues that it would receive if workers earned more, not to mention the sales taxes if they had more to spend and future income taxes if they had money to invest.

The government also has to pay for welfare programs, food stamps, and other supplemental income because people can't earn a living wage. A living minimum wage would provide a huge incentive for people on welfare to get jobs and, in some cases, might actually allow them to afford day-care programs that they must have in order to work. If corporate America paid a living wage of $10 an hour (or $9 an hour if health care is provided), taxpayers wouldn't need to subsidize business labor practices with all these poverty programs.

(continued)

> Crime is also reduced by a higher minimum wage because the unskilled workers who have trouble finding a job tend to be the ones drawn to a life of crime, despite the risks. A higher minimum wage makes legitimate jobs more appealing because it's possible to make a decent living.
>
> "Free marketeers" claim that a higher minimum wage hurts poor people by eliminating jobs. Yet the disasters predicted each time the minimum wage rises never seem to happen. After the minimum wage was raised in the 1990s, the economy registered record growth, and the unemployment rate fell. One reason is that many people currently must work two jobs to stay afloat. A higher minimum wage would allow these workers to survive on one job and spend more time helping their families and communities, thereby freeing up jobs for the unemployed. Because corporate America has effectively crushed union organizing, low-income workers need a living minimum wage to be in a fair bargaining position with employers.

Presto: the left becomes the instrument of smaller government. The earned-income tax credit is flawed in many ways. It requires the nuisance of filling out extra forms; the poor get their money back a year after they earn a salary (and must pay high interest rates on loans to get by until then); the danger of tax fraud is much greater; and the incentive for the underground economy is enhanced (because earnings beyond a minimal level reduce the EITC, whereas a tax cut reduces the incentive for hidden earnings).

In many urban areas, the burgeoning payday loan companies offer the working poor short-term loans at about 500 percent annual interest so that they can pay their bills until the next payday. If progressives could lower taxes on the working poor and the middle class, they would have enough money to start saving, investing, and spending more effectively, instead of wasting resources just trying to keep their heads above water. For the rich, a small tax cut may mean the difference between buying a slightly more expensive new car or adding a few thousand to their plentiful stock accounts. For the poor, a small tax cut may mean the difference in whether they can afford to go to college or get health insurance. And because the poor actually pay only a small part of the nation's tax bill anyway, a substantial tax cut for the majority of the working poor would cost far less than the tax cuts proposed by Republicans and Democrats for the richest Americans.

Because progressives are trapped in the habit of supporting welfare programs rather than seeking benevolent social goals with tax cuts, the image of the left as big-spending liberals rather than tax-cutting progressives is confirmed. Not only would a tax cut for the poor improve the image of the left far more than another welfare program or tax credit, but it would also be more difficult for conservatives to oppose.

Instead of simply advocating higher taxes on the rich to pay for more social programs, progressives need to urge an overall package of tax cuts in which most Americans' taxes are reduced and those of only the top 1 percent are increased. The public's reaction to such a plan would be overwhelmingly positive. If people voted according to self-interest, progressives would get 99 percent support (although unfortunately, 100 percent of the members of Congress and the top-level media would be part of the small elite against the idea).

Progressives lose when the public debate about taxes is framed as a choice between Democrats (moderate tax cuts for the middle class) and Republicans (large tax cuts for the rich). Until progressives can offer an alternative tax cut plan that benefits the working poor, tax cut proposals for the wealthy will dominate political discussions, and progressives will continue to be tagged with the destructive "tax-and-spend" label.

Capital Gains for the Rich

Of all the inequities and insanity in the American tax code, perhaps none is as incomprehensible to a rational tax system as the special tax break for capital gains given to the wealthiest Americans.

An analysis by Citizens for Tax Justice shows that the capital gains tax cut proposed by conservatives would provide an average windfall of nearly $8,000 per year to the richest 1 percent of families, while the average low-income and middle-class taxpayers would save less than $30 a year. The Center for Budget and Policy Priorities estimates that by 2005, a capital gains tax cut would cost $5 billion a year. Far from cutting capital gains, progressives ought to be pushing for an egalitarian tax code under which income and capital gains are taxed equally.

Many progressives make the mistake of attacking the capital gains subsidy in the tax code solely as a "giveaway to the rich." Of course, it is precisely that. But progressive ideas are most persuasive when they don't use the standard rhetoric of attacking the rich. The capital gains subsidy (and the proposal by virtually all Republicans—including Steve Forbes's flat tax—to increase this tax break) can be effectively countered on libertarian, antigovernment grounds. What business is it of the government to judge the value of the way we earn our money? Why should the government impose lower taxes on a stock investor than on a construction worker? Why should the government subsidize the money made in stock market speculation while requiring higher taxes on money invested in a certificate of deposit?

Why should someone who makes his money by investing stocks benefit from a lower tax rate than does the construction worker who goes out and works hard all day to make a living? The construction worker pays more in income taxes than the speculator—and the far right wants the speculator to pay nothing at all.

The reason that the construction worker pays higher taxes in order to subsidize the stock speculator, we are told, is that paper shufflers are more important to our economy than construction workers are. Yet there's never been any sound economic theory to prove that $50,000 made on Wall Street is more important to our economy than $50,000 made on Main Street. However, the economists who argue for a lower capital gains tax, and the politicians who embrace it, are all close friends with the people who profit from the idea.

Take the case of George W. Bush. In 1998, he made millions from selling his stake in the Texas Rangers—turning a $640,000 investment into $15.4 million with the help of $130 million in corporate welfare payments from taxpayers for a new stadium. But Bush paid only $3.7 million in taxes (about 20 percent of his income) owing to the low capital gains tax rate. If Bush had earned his income rather than obtaining it through an investment, he would have paid millions more in taxes. Why does selling a baseball team entitle Bush to a special tax break that somebody selling insurance couldn't receive?

Conservatives argue that capital gains cuts are important to create economic growth. Considering that these same economists argue for any tax cut on the same grounds, there doesn't seem to be any particular reason to favor a capital gains tax cut over an income tax cut, except that because the richest Americans "earn" most of the capital gains. This kind of tax cut targets the people who give the most money to politicians.

Isn't it interesting that the advocates of "tax simplification" suddenly want more complicated taxes when it comes in the form of a tax break for the rich? After all, keeping capital gains income separate from other forms of income only complicates people's taxes—unless, of course, the "simplify" tax debate is just a cover for cutting taxes on the wealthy.

The low tax rate on capital gains also distorts the economy. Instead of investing in safe bonds or CDs (which pay interest taxed as income) or stable, profitable companies (which provide dividends taxed at the higher income rate), many investors seek high-risk, unprofitable companies that provide no dividends but have the potential to rise in value and create the desirable low-taxed capital gains. The stock market is precarious enough without the government providing handouts to the people taking the biggest risks.

The principle of fairness in taxation demands a reformed tax code that lowers income taxes (especially for the poor) while providing for equality between income and capital gains taxes. By challenging the current tax structure that favors the wealthy and the powerful, progressives could take away one of the most powerful and popular issues manipulated by conservatives. But even more important, the left could use tax policy and tax cuts to help the poor more than any government program could accomplish. Until progressives address tax cuts, they will always find themselves on the losing end of American politics.

Chapter 10

MAKING CRIME A
PROGRESSIVE ISSUE

Progressives have a reputation for being soft on crime. You'll usually find the left protesting an act of police brutality or complaining about too many prisons or opposing the death penalty and the war on drugs.

All of these issues are worthy ones, but together they give the impression that the left doesn't care about crime. Yet progressives actually far more devoted to stopping crime than conservatives are, but because the right more effectively uses anticrime rhetoric, the public views them as the political equivalent of Sergeant Joe Friday.

Conservatives aren't tough on crime: they're stupid on crime. Just as is the case with "small government," conservatives only want to be "tough" on certain criminals—the poor, dark skinned, and powerless. Conservatives stand firmly opposed to tough laws when it comes to tax evasion, date rape, corporate crime, many violent crimes, police brutality, gun control, and much more. By supporting mandatory minimum penalties for nonviolent drug crimes, the right has clogged the legal system with offenders who have not committed serious crimes. As a result, violent offenders are more difficult to pursue, prosecute, and imprison when so much time is spent by police, prosecutors, judges, and prisons taking care of minor drug dealers.

Rape is one of worst crimes ignored by the right; a rational criminal knows that it's far better under the American legal system to sexually assault a woman than to carry even a small amount of crack. The chance of a conviction for rape is small, and the penalties are often remarkably light for a violent crime. More than half of convicted rapists serve less than one year in jail, and the vast majority are never even arrested. Of all the violent crimes committed in America, rape is by far the least punished. When it comes to rape, conservatives are willing to accept a system in which women can easily be attacked without consequences—and then condemn a tough stand on rape as a feminist crusade for an imaginary problem.

The right also serves as apologists for white-collar criminals. America puts far more shoplifters than corporate crooks in prison, even though the economic cost of white-collar crime is enormous. A man who shoplifts a candy bar in Texas gets a sixteen-year sentence, while corporate criminals steal millions from the public with almost no danger of spending time in jail. Corporate crime goes virtually unpunished, whereas mandatory sentences put nonviolent drug dealers (and drug users) behind bars for long periods of time.

Even the Internal Revenue Service discriminates against the poor. The IRS used to audit the rich about ten times as often as the poor, but today a person making less than $25,000 has one in seventy-four chances of being audited, versus one in eighty-seven chances for someone who makes more than $100,000.

Worse yet, conservatives want symbolic policies on crime rather than effective public policy. They build more prisons and push mandatory death penalties for federal crimes like mutilating a postal carrier, but they refuse to invest in the education, drug rehabilitation, and jobs programs that have proved to be the most effective anticrime measures.

From 1982 to 2000, the number of people in American prisons grew from 300,000 to more than 2 million. If you throw in the people on parole or probation, it exceeds 5 million. The huge costs of this police state make going to Harvard seem like a bargain. Building one prison bed costs more than $50,000; incarcerating one prisoner costs about $25,000 per year.

The prison boom has come at a price: America is sacrificing its schools, colleges, and social programs to pay the high cost of imprisoning almost 1 percent of its population. Since 1987, spending on prisons has grown by more than 30 percent while higher education has been cut by 18 percent. In 1995, for the first time, state spending in America on prison construction exceeded spending on university construction.

Overcrowded prisons contribute to crime because the underground culture of drugs, rape, and violence proliferates in a climate where the idea of rehabilitation is dismissed as a liberal fantasy. We throw younger and younger teens into prisons, which have become colleges for criminality, graduating dangerous youths who are trained to do nothing but commit more crimes. The right resists the idea of educating prisoners because it would raise embarrassing questions about why our society doesn't provide quality education for these people before they turn to a life of crime.

As a social investment, the current prison system is one of the worst economic decisions we can make. If half the money spent on arresting, prosecuting, and imprisoning Americans was instead devoted to better schools, scholarships to college, alcohol and drug treatment programs, rehabilitation, and improved job opportunities, we would do more to stop crime in America than all the Supermax prisons combined. Instead, we have created an insane cycle of prisons begetting crime that do little to make us safer and impose enormous human and economic costs.

Our obsession with prisons also exacerbates America's continuing race problem. Less than 15 percent of Americans are black, but 46 percent of prisoners are African American. One-third of all black men in their twenties are currently in the justice system. The drug war has especially intensified the race gap in criminal prosecutions by imposing heavy mandatory sentences for nonviolent drug crimes. Most drug convictions are of blacks—in the Chicago area, 90 percent of the drug offenders in jail are black, and less than 1 percent are white. Yet African Americans are actually less likely than whites to use illegal drugs. According to the National Household Survey on Drug Abuse, about 1.2 percent of whites aged eighteen to twenty-five in America use cocaine, compared with 0.9 percent of blacks the same age—around 220,000 white users that age versus 34,000 black users. Illicit drug use in America is a predominantly white problem, but blacks are the main targets of arrest. It's little wonder that the war on drugs has been a failure: most of the drug users never are threatened by arrest because they're white and well-off.

In a country that continues to have massive residential segregation, an appalling gap between the quality of predominantly white and predominantly black schools, and a massive disparity in wealth and economic opportunity, the criminal justice system still ranks as the key impediment to equality.

Conservatives like to argue that despite the toll in money and human costs, the expansion of prisons has made America safer. Since reaching a peak in 1991, all forms of crime have decreased dramatically, but there is no scientific evidence that the additional number of prisons caused this drop in crime. If prisons stop crime, then violence wouldn't have continued rising throughout the prison-building boom of the 1980s.

Poverty and guns are by far the biggest reasons for the persistence of crime. As any economist can tell you, the incentives to commit crime increase when many people are poor. When a small number of Americans become very rich (as happened in the 1980s) while the poor grew poorer, the incentive to steal rises, as does the sense of injustice fueled by the widening gap between rich and poor. When the sheer number of very poor people escalates rapidly (as it did during the 1980s), a rise in crime is likely. Conservative critics like to blame video games for the crime, but TV shows like *Lifestyles of the Rich and Famous*, commercials for government lottery games, and news coverage of Donald Trump may have had more to do with the growth in crime. When a nation puts millionaires on a pedestal, as America did in the decades of greed, it creates a desire for wealth that most people can fulfill only through criminal activity.

From 1979 to 1992, a period of growth in crime, poverty in America climbed. The proportion of men (who are the most likely criminals) with low earnings (below $13,091 in 1992 dollars) nearly doubled, from 7.7 percent to 14.1 percent. The proportion of young people aged eighteen to twenty-four (again, a large part of the potential criminal population) with low earnings more than doubled, from 22.9 percent to 47.1 percent. From 1973 to 1993, real hourly wages for men without a high school degree fell 27.1 percent; for male high school graduates, the wages fell 20.2 percent. Together, these two groups made up half the male workforce. Despite the tremendous growth of the very poor, the proportion of very rich Americans (above $52,364 in earnings) also grew, from 16.3 percent to 18.1 percent, only increasing the envy and the incentive for robbery. This doesn't mean that poor people are only the criminals. White-collar crime committed by the wealthy involves much larger amounts of money, but it's prosecuted less often than petty crime is.

Welfare programs were devastated during the Reagan and Bush administrations, cutting out much of the safety net that might have helped prevent the hopelessness during an economic downturn for the downtrodden. One example of how dumb budget cuts end up costing society more in the long run can be seen in mental health and drug programs. We cut these "social" programs (which really are health programs) and end up spending far more putting drug addicts in jail. Our society has a growing number of prisons but a six-month waiting list for drug treatment. Far more money is allocated to punishment than to solutions. Instead of stopping crime before it happens, America's conservative approach to crime tries to throw more and more Americans into jail. Until rational and effective anticrime measures are instituted, America will continue to have one of the highest crime rates in the developed world.

The Death of the Death Penalty

Like most progressives, I used to think that opposing capital punishment was a hopeless, albeit noble, cause. Throughout my life, polls have always shown that the overwhelming majority of Americans support the death penalty. Politicians rush to embrace executions as the ultimate in the politics of pure symbolism. The closest thing to an electoral death penalty for American political candidates is opposition to capital punishment. Unless you favor killing people, you can kiss your political future good-bye.

The presumption of antiprogressive public opinion is turning out to be dead wrong. When the death penalty is widely understood as unjust, ineffective, and biased against the poor and dark skinned, the majority of Americans will reject it. As one of the few democratic countries that still murders its citizens, America is behind the rest of the world on a civilization scale. And as a nation with a high crime rate, the death penalty clearly does not discourage criminal activity. Ultimately, the United States will reject capital punishment if the most convincing arguments against it can be heard.

Pointing out the inherent moral evil of executing people is not going to convince a lot of Americans, even if most of the democratic world finds the practice morally abhorrent (dictators, of course, are usually strong advocates of capital punishment). America is too accustomed to crime and violent deaths and sees too many movies in which the good cop blows away the evil criminal. "Make my day" resonates too deeply with the public to make purely moral arguments against the death penalty very effective. But if Dirty Harry is our model of law enforcement, it's because he always kills the bad guys, not innocent citizens. That's where the ideal of the death penalty diverges sharply from reality, and it's the most vulnerable flaw of capital punishment.

Support for capital punishment is widespread but shallow. The first time that a recently executed prisoner is definitively proved innocent, the public's enthusiasm for the death penalty will largely disappear. The corpse of an innocent man leaves an ugly stain.

Already, a number of near misses have shaken public support. In Illinois alone, thirteen death row inmates have been released in recent years—one more than the number of prisoners executed since the death penalty was reinstated in the state in 1977. These were not cases of criminals getting off on technicalities—in fact, the restrictions on appeals have made it nearly impossible for death row inmates to be released because they didn't get a fair trial or their constitutional rights were violated. The Illinois exonerations were examples of actual innocence, proven by DNA evidence or confessions by the true criminals. Some of these innocent men were tortured by electric shock until they confessed to Chicago police officers—and many more torture victims are still being held in prison based on their coerced confessions.

A 1999 *Chicago Tribune* investigation of the death penalty found numerous mistakes in capital cases. In 49 percent of the cases, the death penalty was vacated, and a new trial or sentencing hearing was ordered by appeals courts because of irregularities in the trial. In a third of the cases in which a black defendant was accused of killing a white victim, the trial was decided by an all-white jury—and in one case, prosecutors removed twenty African Americans from the juror pool in order to form an all-white jury. Thirty-three death row inmates in Illinois had been represented by disbarred or suspended attorneys. As Illinois Supreme Court Justice Moses Harrison II explained, "The system is not working. Innocent people are being sentenced to death."

Illinois is not exceptional, except in the attention given to the problem of innocent people being executed. Most other states with the death penalty still have innocent individuals on death row. Illinois was unusual in having strong activists working on the cause, and exceptional individuals such as the Northwestern University professor David Protess, who assigned his journalism students the task of investigating death row cases, resulting in the release of several innocent men. If every journalism school and law school in America required its students to investigate a death penalty case, the news would be filled with stories of innocent people who had been executed or held on death row. And the popular support for the death penalty would disappear in the face of its unjust and unequal impact.

Following the public outcry, Illinois Republican Governor

George Ryan ordered a moratorium on the death penalty, declaring that "our system in this state was absolutely broken," and appointed a panel to investigate how the state could avoid executing innocent people, a move that Bill Clinton praised as "courageous" and then, not surprisingly, refused to follow.

Governor Ryan declared, "Until in my mind it's flawless, there won't be any death penalty." No legal system is perfect: there will always be innocent people in prison, and as long as there is a death penalty, there is a high probability of the government's executing someone who has not committed a crime. Without a death penalty, though, there is always an opportunity for a mistake to be corrected and an innocent person to be released. With the death penalty, mistakes in the legal system are permanent—and fatal.

The polls in Illinois showed a dramatic drop in support for the death penalty following the revelations about innocent prisoners on death row. As in every other poll, the wording of the question determines the response. A *Chicago Tribune* poll found that if the alternative of "life in prison without chance of parole" was offered to the respondents, support for the death penalty dropped from a thirty-point lead to a virtual dead heat with a ban on state executions.

A Columbia University study found that 68 percent of death penalty cases in America had been overturned during the appeals process because of trial errors. From bad judges and incompetent public defenders to prosecutors who withheld evidence and witnesses who lied, most defendants convicted of a capital crime did not receive a fair trial in America. Examining more than 5,000 judicial decisions covering every finalized capital conviction and appeal in the United States between 1973 and 1995, the Columbia study found serious, reversible errors in 68 percent of the cases. The mistakes were not mere technicalities but included egregiously incompetent defense lawyers (37 percent); prosecutorial misconduct, often the suppression of evidence of innocence (19 percent); and faulty instructions by judges to jurors (20 percent). In 82 percent of the cases in which the error was corrected, the defendants did not receive a death sentence on review, and in 7 percent of these cases, they were found not guilty.

These numbers do not reflect all the mistakes made in capital cases, as the Columbia study looked only at the courts' final decisions about errors in these cases. In reality, the proportion of not guilty persons sentenced to death (about 5 percent) or those not deserving a death sentence (more than half) is probably even larger than the Columbia study discovered. These figures also don't include a potentially large number of convicted individuals who slip through the system and are executed because of the efforts to close "loopholes" and prevent anyone from invoking such errors or actual innocence. The system of executions in America is sufficiently broken that many examples of prosecutorial misconduct, judicial errors, and inadequate defense never are heard about or endorsed by the appeals system.

The notion of killing innocent men turned many notable conservatives against the death penalty. Pat Robertson declared his support for a moratorium, as did George Will, who noted that the number of exonerated death row inmates creates "a reasonable inference that innocent people have been executed."

It's often cheaper to keep someone in prison than to execute him, owing to the high cost of the appeal process. The public has a choice: we can either spend a lot of money to make sure that innocent people are not executed, or we can shrug our shoulders and accept the fact that some innocent people will be murdered by the government in the name of law and order.

Given the lengthy process in the courts before an execution—a necessary system if the deaths of innocent people at our hands are to be avoided—it can often take decades before a death sentence is finally carried out. According to the Columbia Law School study, it took an average of nine years to finalize capital decisions—whether death, imprisonment, or release—owing to the lengthy appeals necessary to resolve all the errors.

Many government executions are actually a form of state-assisted suicide, since many people go to the electric chair only because they have given up their appeals and consider a quick death preferable to spending the rest of their lives in prison. Granting the wishes of suicidal convicts and cutting the life span of a few middle-aged prisoners doesn't exactly fulfill the public's desire for revenge embodied by the death penalty.

This lack of fulfillment may be why so many of the world's democracies have outlawed capital punishment. The flaws and dangers of the death penalty far outweigh its imagined benefits. The advocates of capital punishment contend that executing criminals is the only way to be sure they won't commit another crime. Unless conservatives overwhelm prisons with so many nonviolent drug dealers that they have to let the murderers go free, there is no danger posed by a sentence of life in prison. The fear of a death sentence, however, can make a criminal or a prisoner more desperate and willing to harm people. If the death penalty really did stop crime, then America should have one of the lowest crime rates in the world. The fact that an ineffective and unjust policy to execute people continues in the twenty-first century should be a national embarrassment for a civilized country.

Gun Control

By far the most destructive policy pushed by conservatives is their support for widespread and unregulated gun ownership.

It's getting to the point where it's easier to buy a gun than a pack of cigarettes—and more deadly.

Pinko left-wing crackpots are those of us who suggest that the relentless defense of the "right" to own, carry, and use every automatic weapon ever invented just might have something to do with the epidemic of violence in America. Gun control is one of the most popular issues in America today, but the disproportionate power of the National Rifle Association (NRA) over our government prevents any effective national gun regulation.

In their infomercials, the NRA urges the public to fight "armed predators" by joining Charlton Heston's Silver Bullet Brigade and receiving a Charlton Heston silver bullet engraved with his signature. In reality, though, the predators in America are armed largely because of the NRA's policies and the politicians it funds.

Gun control in America hasn't worked, say the opponents. But gun control has never been really tried in America. We have waiting periods and modest restrictions on semiautomatic weapons but nothing to halt the "gun in every pocket" philosophy in America, where guns nearly outnumber people. A few places (such as Chicago or Washington, D.C.) actually ban guns, but a legal gun purchase is available a subway ride away, in a nearby suburb where gun dealers cater to the high-powered needs of street gangs.

A study by the National Economic Research Associates found that in those states with strong gun control laws, 75 percent of the handguns used in crimes came from other states. But in those states with weak gun control laws, two-thirds of the handguns used in crimes were purchased in that state. The states that make it easy to buy a gun not only endanger their own citizens but also export death to people throughout America. In the case of New York, where 90 percent of handguns used in crime come from outside the state, 2,624 handguns used by criminals between 1989 and 1997 were originally sold in Florida, often in bulk quantities. Clearly, criminals do not acquire guns with magical incantations; they buy them at low prices thanks to the ease with which the NRA-supported measures allow handguns to travel from dealer to criminals in a nationwide network.

Gun advocates argue that if guns were restricted, criminals would simply find other weapons. While it's probably true that knife killings would rise if America had effective gun control, the number of murders and other crimes would undoubtedly decrease. It's extraordinarily difficult to rob a bank with a knife, and drive-by knifings tend to be very rare.

Airplanes are a perfect example of how gun control actually works. Apart from a few drunken, obstinate passengers, crime is virtually nonexistent on airplanes, despite the cramped, uncomfortable quarters. Why? The main reason that crime rates are so much lower there than elsewhere is because we effectively prevent people from carrying guns onto planes.

In fact, the rest of the world is a testament to the remarkable effectiveness of gun control. No other single anticrime measure would save America more money and more lives than gun control. Gun advocates are quick to point to Switzerland and Israel as places where a well-armed population does not engage in much criminal activity. But Switzerland and Israel are two of the smallest countries in the world, from which it's extraordinarily difficult to leave (10,000-foot-tall mountains in one case, checkpoints and hostile Arab countries in the other). The Swiss (a traditionally neutral country) and the Israelis (a special case in which a massive police/military presence discourages common crime) have learned over the years to carry guns without killing one another, a fact that has little relevance to America. The fact that the well-armed Swiss don't have a tradition of murder is not a reason to promote a handgun for every American.

All other industrialized democracies, including Japan and

most of Europe, have far lower gun ownership rates, far lower murder rates, and far lower crime rates than the United States. The reasonable approach would be to get rid of the guns until we prove as a nation that we're mature enough to own dangerous weapons without spilling blood all over the place. Until then, opposing gun control in America is like letting every kid carry a switchblade on the theory that Boy Scouts get to have Swiss army knives when they're out in the woods.

The notion that "guns don't kill people, people kill people" would be fine if we didn't have so many people killing one another with guns. It is an irrefutable fact that guns make it much easier to kill people. When guns are restricted, the result is not an epidemic of criminals beating people to death with soup spoons.

The NRA's latest crusade is to return America to the Wild West by permitting concealed handguns to be carried in public. Of course, in some cases, criminals are stopped—or scared off—by armed resistance. But the number of suicides, killings during domestic disputes, or friends and relatives accidentally shot exceeds the number of lives saved by having a gun. More important, the proliferation of guns and the ease of acquiring them in America endanger the entire society by allowing criminals to buy weapons with virtually no restraints.

Being able to carry a concealed gun doesn't discourage crime, even if the gun is used responsibly. Guns simply put criminals in an arms race. If most Americans were carrying concealed handguns, criminals would not stop committing crimes; they'd simply trade up from a knife to a gun themselves. Since criminals almost always have the advantage of surprise, people who carry guns do far more to endanger themselves (and everyone else) than to stop crime. When concealed guns can be legally taken into bars, ball games, and other public spaces, the danger of arguments escalating into deadly fights increases. The consequence of legalizing concealed guns is that the number of crimes often decreases faster in those states that continue to ban the proliferation of guns.

The Right to Deadly Weapons: Misinterpreting the Second Amendment

Oh, but there's that pesky Second Amendment, rapidly recalled by conservatives who oddly seem to forget the rest of the Bill of Rights at a moment's notice. According to a strict interpretation of the Second Amendment, Americans today would be entitled to "gun freedom" only if they were "well-regulated" members of the militia (that is, the National Guard).

The Founding Fathers never imagined that Americans would be given the "right" to own a weapon capable of mass murder. Highly accurate semiautomatic guns (which are designed by gun manufacturers for easy conversion to automatics) with large clips stand in sharp contrast to the inaccurate weapons of the eighteenth century that took a long time to aim and reload. Compared with muskets, today's legal high-powered rifles have the firepower of a cannon, but the Founders never conceived that anyone would have a "right" to own a cannon or haul one around on the public streets.

The earliest citizens of the United States needed to have guns because they were not only the militia but also the armory for the U.S. government, which lacked the resources to buy enough weapons to fight off an invasion. In sum, the Second Amendment was a protection against the disarmament of the United States in the face of foreign enemies.

Today, this reasoning no longer applies. The United States faces no threat of foreign invasion. Our military has plenty of guns to fight our enemies, and these are far more powerful than private weapons. An armed citizenship for patriotism's sake is an anachronism and an increasingly dangerous archaic policy.

The notion that the Second Amendment was designed to help Americans overthrow their own government is absurd. The Founding Fathers feared violent revolts such as Shay's Rebellion. That's why the Second Amendment was not written to make carrying any weapon a fundamental right; it's a right only in the context of "a well-regulated militia."

So, let anyone in the well-regulated militia (armed forces or National Guard) have a well-regulated gun—that is, a weapon that can't be easily concealed, a weapon that can't be easily converted into an automatic, a weapon that can't be sold to criminals via gun shows and flea markets, a weapon that can't be carried around in public, a weapon that can't be bought on the spur of the moment. (As Homer Simpson noted about waiting periods while trying to buy a gun from the Bloodbath & Beyond Gun Shop, "Five days? But I'm mad now.")

Even if having a gun is a fundamental American right, that doesn't prevent sensible regulation. Freedom of speech (which is not burdened by the "well-regulated" requirement of the Second Amendment) has been commonly interpreted to allow limitations such as time, place, and manner restrictions. If we apply this logic to the right to bear arms, it is easy to imagine that the Constitution permits a ban on concealable guns, as well as a ban on guns in urban areas and in most public areas. The manner of guns can also be regulated: banning automatic weapons and cop-killer ammo, requiring gun locks, and compelling gun owners to have a permit. Virtually any taxes and laws regulating the manufacture, distribution, and sale of guns also are constitutional.

Thus, almost any regulation short of banning all guns for all law-abiding citizens would almost certainly be constitutional, depending on the number of Scalia clones appointed to the

Supreme Court in the future. America has never tried serious gun control measures, and there is no reason to believe that public currently supports a total ban. An array of options short of a total ban, though, would help reduce America's deadly over-abundance of weapons.

Instead of worrying about whether it is wrong to follow an ancient Constitution's misguided protections for gun owners, we should concentrate on adopting all the effective, popular, and constitutional types of gun control. If real gun control doesn't stop this country's deadly obsession with guns, perhaps then the public will be ready to consider changing our legal anachronisms. The Constitution isn't killing us, but the cowardice of politicians and the political power of the National Rifle Association are.

Unfortunately, most progressives end up supporting ineffective gun control measures. Optional gun locks, waiting periods, the Brady bill, bans on concealed handguns, and similar efforts all are beneficial, but none of them has had much effect on the widespread distribution of guns in America and the crime that results.

An absolute ban on all guns is unrealistic. There are simply too many guns and too many gun owners in America to make a gun ban feasible, and the most likely reaction would be paranoid private militias hoarding huge numbers of guns to use against federal agents.

The most feasible approach is not an outright ban but effective gun control. All guns should be registered and marked to allow the guns and the bullets shot from them to be traced if linked to a crime. Only strictly controlled gun dealers could sell new guns or buy used ones, with the instant identification (and arrest) of criminals who tried to buy guns or anyone who tried to modify a gun illegally or to sell one that was not registered. If a gun were used in a crime, then the person who originally bought it and illegally sold it should be arrested as an accessory to the crime.

Guns would be allowed for law-abiding citizens in their homes and for strictly regulated activities such as hunting and sport shooting. All gun owners would need to have gun locks and other safety measures to prevent anyone else from using the gun. No one (apart from police and licensed security people) would be allowed to carry a gun in public. Only one gun per year could be purchased by law-abiding citizens, and in order to purchase a gun, they would have to show that they still possessed and had not illegally modified any other guns registered to them.

Effective gun control must do far more to stop crime than symbolism. Until progressives push for stringent controls on the distribution of guns and go beyond the limited steps permitted by the NRA and their politicians, the public will never know that gun control can work.

Chapter 11

WINNING THE CULTURE WARS

Whenever conservatives become particularly desperate, they like to latch onto cultural issues. The far right perceives the culture wars as a winning approach because their economic and social policies favoring the rich have so little popular support. But the truth is that cultural conservatives are even more out of touch with the American people than the economic conservatives are. The culture wars work for the far right only as the politics of distraction. Ultimately, Americans don't want a country dominated by censorship and repression, and progressives don't need to fear a defense of freedom and equal rights.

The First Amendment in Flames

Here's the surest test of whether a politician is a self-serving bureaucrat willing to sacrifice the Constitution for his poll numbers: does this individual support the flag desecration amendment? There are a lot of serious problems facing America and the world, but everyone agrees that flag burning isn't one of them. Politicians don't want to deal with poverty, homelessness, inequality, discrimination, lack of health care, or a thousand different issues—but they're right on top of our deadly flag-burning crisis. (Global warming is probably caused by the noxious fumes emitted from this orgy of flag burning across the country.)

What makes a ban on flag burning problematic is that American flags are supposed to be burned when they become too worn and tattered to use. Thus, what a ban on flag desecration really prohibits is not the act of burning but the intent motivating it. The government cannot get into the business of looking at two people who burn their own flags and deciding that one is patriotic and the other is a criminal. The amendment would ban an attitude, not an act.

Technically, physical flag desecration doesn't stop at burning. It includes leaving a flag out in the dark, allowing a flag to touch the ground, and using the flag in clothing or commercial advertisements. We should find it far more offensive when somebody waves a flag in order to sell a car or get elected than if some bozo with a lighter decides to set it on fire. At least the goofy political protestor realizes that flag might stand for more than making money and political expediency.

Should we ban flag desecration to honor our veterans who fought for the flag? Did veterans fight for the protection of political freedom or for a piece of cloth and the infringement of political freedom? The true symbol of America is not a flag but the Bill of Rights. After all, every country has a flag; it's the nation's constitutional protections that make America unique. The only way we desecrate the flag is by desecrating the Bill of Rights with amendments designed to overturn our basic political rights.

If the flag desecration amendment becomes a part of the Constitution, the American flag will become primarily a symbol for the abridgment of free speech, and to anyone who respects the First Amendment, that's the worst desecration of the flag imaginable.

WHY PROGRESSIVES MUST LOVE FREE SPEECH

The left must stand strongly on the side of free speech. Because there is so much censorship of progressive ideas, it can be tempting for the left to turn the tables and try to silence far right advocates. But repression is unnecessary: progressive ideas are more popular than conservative ones, and all the left needs to do is get a fair and open hearing.

Censorship is not only wrong, it's also a losing strategy for the left. Progressives attract more attention if they're the censors. Because conservative censorship is largely taken for granted, news about intolerance on the right isn't usually publicized. But when someone on the left seems guilty of censorship, the right's publicity machine quickly starts up. That's why the right was able to push the myth of political correctness in the 1990s and invent the idea of a wave of left-wing oppression sweeping college campuses at a time when there was more freedom of thought than ever before, and infringement of free speech on campuses by conservative forces was more prevalent than anything committed by the left.

Progressives certainly need to better publicize incidents of censorship, but the left must also realize that the right will always win the suppression battles. It has all the resources and the media on its side. When some leftists are willing to make exceptions to the First Amendment to silence conservative hate mongers, it becomes even more difficult for progressives to draw attention to the censorship of left-wing ideas. The only winning strategy is to maintain a consistent commitment to freedom of speech.

Censorship and the Arts

New York City Mayor Rudy Giuliani recently threatened to eliminate all city support for the Brooklyn Museum of Art, revoking millions of dollars unless it canceled a British exhibit called "Sensation." This was only the latest in a long line of cases in which conservative politicians punished museums, artists, and the public in order to demand that their values control public subsidies of the arts.

One of the strongest arguments for censorship is the libertarian line: no art should receive public support. It's a lovely theoretical argument, but the fact is that the public supports the arts. The question then becomes, should every institution that accepts any amount of public money be forced to capitulate to the artistic judgments of Rudy Giuliani or Jesse Helms? Nobody elected these guys to be the commanders of the thought police. As for the general issue of government funding, it seems reasonable that if we are willing to publicly fund weapons, schools, parks, highways, libraries, cops, bridges, and trillions of dollars worth of other activities, spending a minuscule part of our taxes on art strikes me as a good thing. The alternative would be for museums to sharply raise their entrance fees, effectively keeping out the poor.

If you pass a law banning public libraries from buying any books with "dirty words" in them (or punish them with budget cuts if they do), that's censorship, even if it only involves removing this "public subsidy" of dirty literature. Censorship is evil not only because it tries to punish artists or writers and the curators or librarians who pay them. Censorship is evil because it seeks to remove certain ideas and works of art from the public view.

The other main argument for censorship is the "offensiveness" line: As Giuliani puts it, "If you are a government-subsidized enterprise, then you can't do things that desecrate the most personal and deeply held views of people in society." In other words, every public institution must be devoted to the uncontroversial, the bland, the intellectual equivalent of baby food. We already have this approach to public tastes in many common areas: it's called Muzak, and it sucks. Maybe worthless crap is the best we can do in elevators, but museums are different. Nobody forces you to enter a controversial exhibit at a museum. If it offends you, leave. If you think it might offend you and the thought of being offended is so horrifying, then stay away from museums. Turn on the sit-coms, and let your brain melt on the floor if it makes you happy. But don't force everybody else to share your desire not to be offended.

Not all art that offends people is good. Some of it's downright awful. But not every book in the public library is a masterpiece, either, and that's not a reason to start a bonfire. The world of art shouldn't be a mausoleum containing only the great art of the past that is deemed acceptable to all (although even Michelangelo's *David* with his exposed penis would probably offend a lot of those congressional art critics). Art (and public support for the arts) must include the potential for controversy, if for no other reason than the fact that it's impossible to make everyone agree.

Progressives often get caught in the trap of defending *Piss Christ* or bullwhips up butts. They need to turn the NEA debate away from particular works of art and into an argument about the importance of diversity. Imagine if public libraries were prohibited from buying controversial books (as some would wish). After all, that's public money subsidizing "offensive" literature.

If an exhibit showing the Virgin Mary with elephant dung can be banned, then certainly a book showing the art in the exhibit could also be banned from the public library. And then, why not all books that insult the Virgin Mary? And since books that discuss sex and contain dirty words offend many people, toss them on the fire, too. After all, why should public money be used to support books and art that might offend someone?

But would you really want to see James Joyce's *Ulysses* or even lesser works of literature banned from our public libraries, or public funding withdrawn because some politician disagrees with a librarian's choice of books? That's what is at stake in the art debate.

Museums and art galleries display an enormous range of art, and public funding is supposed to help these institutions thrive, not to impose Rudy Giuliani's or Jesse Helms's idea of art on the rest of us. Who wants to see paintings of tobacco fields on black velvet?

Of course, no one wants a proliferation of bad art. But if a museum exhibited bad art, nobody would go to see it, and since museums can't rely on public money alone, a museum of bad art would quickly be in trouble. The censors, however, don't want to let the people or the art experts make their judgments; the censors want to tell the rest of us what we can or can't see in our public museums. Conservatives who don't like to be challenged are welcome to open "The Boring Museum for Bland Art That Offends No One" (a title that actually describes quite a few publicly subsidized museums). Far from being obsessed with the cutting edge, agencies such as the NEA and the NEH adhere to a conservative line that usually discourages innovation.

One of the favorite rhetorical tricks of the right is to argue for protection of "the children." Progressives shouldn't evade this argument but counter it head on: it's censorship, not freedom of speech, that hurts our kids and corrupts their minds. The idea that a museum exhibit including dung on the Virgin Mary will turn children into serial killers seems a bit of a stretch. Children see violent acts regularly on TV, cable, and movies; they play video games full of bloody attacks; and they may even see news programs and media coverage about real-life violence, so the negative effects of going to an art museum seem a bit exaggerated in comparison. This doesn't mean we should ban Road Runner cartoons, but it does suggest that the hysteria about "offensive" art and its imagined harm to children must be kept in the proper perspective.

Worst of all, the censors like Giuliani can't see how censorship damages children's minds. When opportunistic politicians try to censor freedom of speech, children learn a powerful lesson: you shouldn't argue with opposing ideas but instead try to eliminate enemy values from public consideration. The lesson taught by Giuliani to our kids is that threats and political intimidation are the proper techniques for winning artistic debates, an idea that is far more dangerous to American values than the worst painting or sculpture imaginable.

Equal Rights for Gays and Lesbians

The key question in the fight over rights for gays and lesbians is whether these rights should be defined as "special" rights or "equal" rights. Contrary to what the homophobes say, there has never been a single proposal for "special rights" to be granted to gays and lesbians. The laws banning discrimination based on sexual orientation apply to all people, gay and straight alike. If an antistraight boss starts firing heterosexuals, they're protected. But everyone knows that there's no danger of gay gangs going around attacking straight people or companies firing people for being attracted to the opposite sex. Equal rights do protect all people, but only gays and lesbians face special attacks for what they do in the bedroom.

No one is arguing that heterosexuals should be banned from marrying each other or that straight people should be thrown out of the army. The "special rights" claim is nothing but a lie. Only equal rights are at stake in this debate.

The religious right likes to say "love the sinner, hate the sin," which usually translates to "spout sanctimonious rhetoric while supporting discrimination." In a free society, if you hate a sin, you try to convince people to stop sinning; you don't demand discrimination against the sinners.

Then there's the infamous pedophilia argument, which says that if we give equality to gays and lesbians, then the next step will be to recognize the rights of pedophiles. There's only one problem with this logic: most pedophiles are straight. Equal rights for adults who have sex with adults doesn't have any logical connection with the "right" of adults to have sex with children. If it did, then we'd have to ban heterosexuality, too, and imagine all the problems that would cause.

For some odd reason, many lukewarm supporters of equal rights (such as Bill Clinton or Al Gore) draw a line at gay marriage. But legal marriage is a civil institution, not a religious one (in fact, a marriage conducted in a church by a minister without the proper paperwork isn't recognized by the government).

Advocates for equality have much more success in urging "civil unions" for gays and lesbians than in using the inflammatory term "gay marriage." Obviously, "civil union" is a compromise, but the fight for "gay marriage" ultimately has to be won church by church, congregation by congregation. A "civil union" approach ends the larger issue of government discrimination.

The problem is that the word *marriage* has two meanings. The religious meaning of marriage conveys God's direct endorsement of the joining of a man and a woman. To some deeply religious people, marriage is a minister in a church clutching a Bible who officiates at an eternal union, and the notion of two lesbians walking down the aisle of their church to get hooked up is abhorrent.

The civil meaning of marriage simply conveys the government's recognition of a union between two people. No religious belief or ceremony or approval is needed to get married; in fact, people whose church explicitly prohibits their marriage (such as divorced Catholics who do not have an annulment) can be married in the eyes of the state. No one can force a church to recognize a marriage. But no one believes that the government should deny divorced Catholics the right to marry again. It's none of the state's business, and the same applies to gay marriages. If marriage were a sacred institution, they wouldn't let Hugh Hefner try it several times. Since a mass conversion of gays and lesbians to heterosexuality seems remarkably unlikely, why not recognize and encourage their lifelong commitments?

The key to winning the debate over "gay marriage" is to separate the religious and civil concepts. That's why the phrase "civil union" is so crucial to an effective argument. A civil union will never threaten the religious concept of marriage. Rather, the civil union changes the turf for the debate: instead of making it seem as if gays and lesbians are imposing homosexuality on the religious institution of marriage, the antigay forces become the ones pushing the government to intrude on and judge a private relationship. While civil union won't persuade the homophobic core who oppose any equal rights for gays and lesbians, it can help turn a losing issue into a winning one simply with the turn of a phrase.

The Abortion Wars

While many of the culture wars are fought over trivial and sometimes comical topics, the question of abortion is very serious. To compel any woman to have a child against her will is completely wrong, as is the intimidation and violence of terrorists within the antiabortion movement who try to deny women the right to choose.

Nevertheless, progressives often lose support for their pro-choice position by focusing solely on protecting the right to have an abortion. Feminists also need to advocate ways to reduce the need for abortions in order to strengthen the public's support for choice.

Both advocates and opponents of abortion rights face the difficult reality that human life is a continuum from fertilization to birth, with no magic moment when humanity appears. For the "prolife" movement, the absolute prohibition of abortion logically means that birth control devices are a form of murder—an idea that even most Catholics don't endorse. For the "prochoice" movement, the absolute right to abortion logically means that the time between legal abortion and illicit murder is the moment when the baby first emerges from the womb—again, a difficult piece of logic for most people.

The success of any argument about abortion, then, usually is determined by where along this nine-month trip the battleground is chosen. The prolifers won when they turned the debate to the so-called partial-birth abortion technique near the end of it: here, abortion rights advocates were trapped into defending an extraordinarily rare procedure conducted very late in pregnancy that bore a disturbing similarity to the birth process itself.

The prochoice movement made the mistake of believing in the domino theory. Advocates of abortion rights are afraid that any ban on a kind of abortion would have a domino effect. But it would have been far better to concede the point and let the prolife movement have its trivial victory by supporting a ban on "partial-birth" abortion except when the health of the woman might be endangered, rather than threatening laws that impede a far wider range of abortions and diverting public attention from important concerns about the access of poor women to abortion. The lesson is that progressives must debate crucial issues with passion and not get sidetracked to issues where the far right has the advantage.

Progressives need to argue that abortion is similar to poverty: we must end the conditions that cause it, not punish the people who must deal with it. It's true that fewer women will have abortions if it's difficult to obtain one, just as fewer people will be on welfare if we punish its recipients and make it difficult to obtain. But progressives must point out that these aren't solutions to the real problems: a woman burdened with an unwanted child is likely to end up in a situation of abuse and poverty. What we need are ways to end abortion by stopping the underlying causes, not by tossing women and doctors into prison.

The first step is to prevent and harshly punish sexual assault, which is a common cause of unwanted pregnancies and also creates enormous moral dilemmas for women opposed to abortion who relive the trauma of a sexual assault throughout their pregnancy. A war on rape even one-half the size of the war on drugs would greatly increase the safety of women and help reduce the number of abortions, a cause that conservatives and progressives ought to agree on. Imagine what would happen if we had a war on rape similar to the antidrug war: antirape commercials on TV, harsh mandatory prison sentences for rapists, antirape programs in every school, and antirape police task forces. (And unlike drug possession, rape is a real crime causing harm to another person, and everyone agrees it should be punished; no one ever calls for the "legalization of rape.") If progressives want to be tough on crime and help reduce the number of abortions without punishing innocent women, a war on rape is the most popular—and effective—stand they can ever take.

The second step is to make birth control and accurate sex education widely available. Telling kids not to have sex is fine (albeit mostly ineffective), but it becomes dangerous when "teaching abstinence" requires a ban on telling teenagers the truth about sex. In reality, teenagers aren't having more sex than they used to—marriage at a young age was simply more common in the good old days. There is no national crisis in sexual morality, only a problem in educating teens to use birth control if they're sexually active. To paraphrase a famous slogan: condoms don't cause teenage sex, hormones cause sex. Making condoms scarce may cause some teens to avoid sex, but so would prison sentences for fornication and the forced wearing of scarlet letters. Yet we wouldn't accept harsh penalties for the "crime" of sex, even if a prison term were an effective way to increase the number of virgins. Then why should anyone advocate punishing girls with unwanted pregnancies and sexually transmitted diseases in order to discourage teen sex?

The third step is to make adoption a more effective and workable system. Instead of the current expensive and ineffective privatized system, a flexible, publicly sponsored system could give women who do not want an abortion the option of adoption on their own terms as well as improving the situation for families seeking children to adopt.

Of course, none of these measures will dissuade the antiabortion extremists. No matter how many abortions are performed, some crackpots will continue to wage their terrorist campaign to bomb clinics and murder doctors, and like other violent terrorists, they must be stopped. Likewise, the nonviolent antiabortion crusaders will continue their opposition to abortion even if the number of fetuses is reduced. The majority of the American people feel ambivalent about abortion. If strong efforts are made to prevent unwanted pregnancies and provide alternatives to abortion, most people will actually be more likely to support abortion rights. It's the large number of abortions—not the need for some women to have them—that bothers most Americans. Therefore, the top goal for progressives must be to reduce the number of abortions in order to increase support for the right to have one.

No one is an advocate of abortion. It's more physically and emotionally painful than effective contraception and more expensive, and it also raises moral issues for many people. Winning the argument about abortion rights requires working to stop abortions while keeping the attention focused on danger of letting the government control anyone's body.

Chapter 12

EQUALITY FOR EVERY CHILD

Reforming Education

Education: no issue holds so much promise for progressives and yet is so dominated by conservative arguments. Education is one of the top priorities for many voters, but most of the debates center on vouchers and privatization and testing.

UNIVERSAL CHILD CARE

A century ago, kindergarten was virtually unknown in America, as it was assumed that parents would take care of their children until they were old enough for formal schooling. But values changed, and kindergarten became a universal part of the American school system as the need for additional schooling grew.

Today, early childhood education is more important than ever, but the American schooling system remains locked in an archaic

---

model. Although most women are in the workforce, our educational structure assumes that women will be able to care for their children constantly until they enter kindergarten.

Universal child care is essential not only to allow women to pursue careers but also to improve the quality of education at a critical period in child development. Most academic research indicates that the preschool ages are crucial to future educational success, but early education is dramatically underfunded compared with more advanced levels of education. Most child-care workers receive barely above the minimum wage, and the government oversight of child-care centers is weak. Until the American commitment to education increases, we will fail to provide our children with the best possible teaching at an early age.

Our schools are failing us, and progressives need to take the lead in urging reform. When progressives simply oppose school vouchers without offering a significant change in the educational system, they give the rhetorical advantage to the right wingers. Defending the current school system not only undermines progressives' credibility, but it also makes it difficult to enact genuinely progressive reforms.

School choice (that is, vouchers) is appealing to many people: Since vouchers have never before been tried on a large scale, predictions of disaster sound excessively apocalyptic to people who are understandably frustrated with the flaws of the public school system.

While vouchers have been the subject of a vigorous public debate over the past two decades, progressive alternatives to the status quo haven't received any attention. The best way to fight school choice is not by fear mongering but by proposing the alternatives of progressive reforms and equalizing funding for all public schools.

The inequality of schools causes a basic problem with vouchers: the best public and private schools in the country are found in wealthy areas, and they don't want poor kids (especially poor black kids) in their schools. The proposed $4,500-a-year vouchers (or often less, depending on the plan) would funnel some money to the Catholic schools and to rich for-profit schools, but they wouldn't fundamentally change the school system.

The rich suburban public schools and private schools aren't going to open their doors to a bunch of poor black kids for a few thousand dollars a year. In fact, they probably wouldn't open those doors very wide for any amount of money. Meanwhile, the loss of funding will further damage urban public schools, which will lose both the funding and their best students, who will be lured to other schools. Instead of improving the educational system, the voucher plan will only exacerbate the inequalities that have devastated schools. The advocates of vouchers are taking a short cut. They're saying that the magic of the free market can revolutionize the educational system without having to add a single dime.

A public education system with genuine freedom of choice would have the following two elements: equal funding for all schools (plus cost-of-living adjustments, special-education students, and the high operating expenses faced by decrepit schools in the inner city) and open access to any school by any student. In other words, a kid in the projects could attend the best school in the richest suburb if he or she wanted to. But what would happen if everyone went to the top schools? The same thing that happens now: the schools would get bigger until they were forced to hold a lottery for admission, and then the district would build another school to accommodate the crowd.

Why won't a "school choice" idea like this be considered? Because the Republicans promoting vouchers only want to destroy the public schools in the inner city; they don't want to threaten the well-financed public schools in the suburbs.

A popular argument among conservatives is that "money doesn't matter." This argument, of course, applies only to public schools, not the Defense Department or corporate welfare. According to the right wingers, the amount of money doesn't affect the quality of schools. If more money is spent on schooling, the funding will simply dissipate into the air, or so the theory goes. For people whose fundamental "free market" ideology depends on individuals responding to financial incentives, the right's "money doesn't matter" argument seems contradictory.

As economic segregation in housing increases, the split between rich towns and poor towns—and the gap between schools—is increasing. The principle of "separate but equal" rejected by the U.S. Supreme Court in *Brown v. Board of Education* still reigns supreme in American schools, except that most states don't bother trying for the equal part. Wealthy, predominantly white public schools receive far more money than do others in America. The students with all these advantages who succeed go to public and private elite universities, which receive far more public money than do the less prestigious colleges.

Conservatives like to cite two important facts from the past thirty years of schooling: the increasing cost of public schools and the declining SAT scores. But conservatives are making two factual mistakes: the fixed costs of schooling have increased in recent years, and the proportion of students taking the SAT has increased.

ATTACKING THE SAT

Many progressives attack the SAT and other standardized tests as racist and sexist. Even though the SAT has a legacy of racism and

(continued)

often gets used in racist ways to deprive blacks and Latinos of educational opportunities, the test itself is not racist. Rather, the American school system is racist. The SAT simply reflects the inequality of our schools and our society.

The real reason to oppose the SAT (and any similar standardized test) is that it has been dumbed down. The SAT bears no resemblance to how the world actually works. Real writers don't use obscure words or odd analogies. Real literature doesn't come in 250-word excerpts. Real mathematicians and engineers need to go far beyond the simple algebra and geometry tested by the SAT. And the SAT ignores the rest of the world: history, science, and much more.

Standardized testing is giving poor kids the worst of both worlds: on the one hand, they can't compete with the kids in rich schools who almost invariably have testing coaches to help them, and on the other hand, schools for poor kids are starting to turn their curricula into test-cramming sessions rather than educating students.

Per-pupil spending on U.S. public schools climbed from about $2,000 per student in 1960 to $6,000 in 1990 (it has remained level since then). The main expense in schools is teaching labor, and teachers' salaries grew from $27,206 to $39,451 in constant dollars, whereas the number of pupils per teacher fell by a third. This large investment in education is one reason that economic growth in America since 1960 has been so dramatic. Critics fail to understand the two main reasons for the higher cost of education: teaching the handicapped and women's equality. In the past, many disabled children were left behind, and today's efforts to educate handicapped children is both morally right and a good investment in the future. But it's very expensive and actually hurts the test scores of public schools, since the successful students often end up being put in regular classes and taking standardized tests such as the SAT.

For most of this century, American schools had the advantage of a well-educated, captive labor source: women who couldn't get other jobs. When women gained access to other jobs, many of them no longer went into teaching. Therefore, in order to attract the same quality of teachers today, schools must pay more money and offer better working conditions, such as smaller classes. Even larger salaries are insufficient to attract potential teachers away from better-paying careers in law or business. The presence of women throughout the U.S. economy has been responsible for much of the increasing productivity in the economy, but a necessary cost of luring well-qualified women away from teaching is that our schools must pay a higher price to compete in the free market. Unfortunately, the expansion in school spending hasn't been sufficient to make up for this higher labor expense, and better-qualified teachers still aren't being lured to the profession of education.

As expectations rise and school funding remains inadequate, public schools are turning to private sources—most often corporations—for badly needed money and school equipment. The growth of corporate control in American schools is a particularly alarming development, given the lack of public support. Chris Whittle's Channel One broadcasts put commercials in front of the eyes of millions of students, with strict rules to prohibit teachers from trying to do any teaching while these corporate ads are occupying classroom time. Whittle even tried to expand his empire to include private, for-profit schools that utterly failed to compete with public schools.

Instead of more commercialization, more dumbed-down testing, and more bureaucracy, schools need to imitate the success of American colleges. By most standards, American elementary and secondary schools don't compete well in the world: the United States has a smaller percentage of high school graduates than do most other developed countries, and it appears that the students in other countries learn more by the time they graduate. Yet American universities are unquestionably the best in the world: most of the advanced research goes on in American labs, all the top students from around the world want to study in America, and far more Americans attend college than do the citizens of any other country.

If we want to improve American schools, we ought to imitate the best aspects of American colleges. This means getting rid of the standardized tests and curricula, trusting teachers' judgment, and allowing them the freedom to teach. This means getting rid of automatically granting tenure but giving tenure to teachers who prove their competence to colleagues. This means getting rid of all-powerful principals and letting teachers make educational decisions.

TEACHING EVOLUTION

More than a century after Darwin, and seventy-five years after the Scopes "monkey" trial, attempts to stop the teaching of evolution in public schools persist. Representative Tom DeLay (R-Tex.) even blamed the mass murder at Columbine High School in Littleton, Colorado, on the teaching of evolution, declaring that the killings were due to the fact that "our school systems teach the children that they are nothing but glorified apes who are evolutionized out of some primordial soup of mud."

DeLay isn't the only creationist with his appendix in a knot. The Oklahoma Textbook Committee even tried to put warning stickers on science textbooks that declared: "No one was present when life first appeared on Earth. Therefore, any statement about life's origins should be considered theory, not fact." Of course, since no one was present when light was emitted from the distant stars, the idea that the night sky is a map of the universe rather than, say, bright lights created by God for his amusement, must be regarded as a theory rather than a fact.

Because most people don't understand what "evolution" or "theory" means, an effective analogy is needed. Evolution is not a theory. It's a fact, like gravity. Scientists have the same certainty that creatures evolve as they do that gravity exerts a force on us. Scientists also have a theory of the complex mechanisms involved in evolution (and in gravity and most other scientific concepts). Scientific ignorance or differences of opinion about some details in the theory of evolution cannot repudiate a basic scientific truth: evolution is a fact.

Religion is not incompatible with the theory of evolution, any more than religion is incompatible with the "theory" that the Earth is spherical. Certain ignorant religious figures at various points in history have considered scientific truth to be dangerous, even when it does not actually contradict the Bible. But if we teach science and not thirteenth-century religious doctrines in the public schools, then we have an obligation to tell the truth. If a bunch of astrologers took over a school and started demanding that the "theory" of astrology be given equal time in public schools alongside scientific evidence about the structure of the universe, no one would take those crackpots seriously. The power of religious fundamentalism in America, however, determines that evolution will be treated as a dangerous idea.

Respecting and trusting successful teachers will improve the quality of teaching, and it will also help schools recruit and retain teachers. It's hard enough to find people willing to enter a low-paid, high-stress profession. But if teachers are denied the intangibles of autonomy and respect, it will be nearly impossible to keep the best ones.

A progressive approach to education can admit the failings of our schools while still refusing to accept the conservative demands to turn over schools to corporations and religious groups. A progressive school system, based on equal opportunity and respect for students, has never been tried in America. Instead, public schools are largely funded by a property tax based on the wealth of the surrounding community. Progressives need to offer more than simply a more fair and just system; they must convince the public that this approach to education will raise standards and improve the efficiency of schools more than will the conservatives' efforts to abandon public schools and rely on dumbed-down tests to reward corporations. A progressive school system cannot rely on the status quo; it must prove to be a success at reforming education in America.

SUPPORTING PRAYER IN SCHOOLS

Progressives are sometimes perceived as hostile to religion because of their belief in the separation of church and state, but the opposite is true. Every child ought to be free to pray in public schools. Despite what many people think, every child is in fact free to pray—individually or in groups—at every public school. Unfortunately, students have very few rights recognized by the U.S. Supreme Court—public schools can censor their newspapers, tell them what clothes to wear, and search them at any time—but the First Amendment clearly prohibits any school from preventing them from praying.

The free exercise of religion isn't an absolute right—a student can't skip a quiz in order to spend an hour praying for a better grade. But public schools can't—and don't—stop students from praying during their free time. What the religious right demands is the "right" to have government-ordered prayer in public schools. They want public school officials to tell students when to pray and what to say.

The biggest problem with school-ordered prayer is deciding what to say. Should students be asked to repeat the words of fundamentalists like Bob Jones who consider Catholics to be Satanists? Or would an inane, nondenominational, inoffensive prayer really satisfy anyone who thinks religion should be meaningful?

Progressives and most believers are united in their suspicion of the government's telling people what to think. If the government can order group prayers, then the threat to religious freedom is far greater than the current protection of the individual student's right to pray. The ideal is simple: ban school-sponsored prayers but allow all students to pray in the manner that their religious conscience dictates. The only threat to religious freedom in schools comes from the religious right's goal of imposing a fundamentalist prayer on students.

Chapter 13

FIGHTING THE UNION LABEL

Labor on the Left

Americans look at unions the same way they look at schools: their own specific unions and schools are fine, but the labor movement overall and public schools in general are regarded as evil. Much of the blame for this belongs to the campaigns pushed by antiunion corporations and media conglomerates, which hate labor with a vengeance. But the labor movement itself deserves a share of the blame, since it's too often concerned with protecting jobs at any cost rather than creating a fair and equitable workplace or building a larger prolabor movement.

The labor movement faces obsolescence at a time when it is more essential than ever. In the global marketplace, corporate exploitation of workers is on the rise. Unions, the primary protection for workers, today are the victims of global outsourcing:

companies simply can destroy unions by moving operations to another country where unions are effectively banned by the government's failure to protect workers' rights. Even in America, the right of workers to organize without suffering retaliation is rarely protected. Anyone who wants to start a union in the United States must do so with the realization that future promotions and job security will be put in serious jeopardy.

Unfortunately, unions are often labeled as corrupt, conservative, protectionist, and out of date. Instead of protecting workers, unions have spent millions giving illicit donations to the Democrats, who ignore the concerns of working people at every turn. That's one reason that the right to unionize is more popular than the labor unions themselves.

Progressives can't do the work of labor organizing. But they can support policies ensuring that unions have a fair shot at surviving the twenty-first century. By advocating policies that help protect workers' rights, progressives can best help the labor movement.

One of the top progressive priorities is raising the minimum wage. A higher minimum wage protects unionized companies from the incentive to abandon union labor in favor of cheaper unorganized workers. When all workers must be paid a living wage, skilled and knowledgeable workers—the core of the labor constituency—become more valuable to companies.

Another progressive priority is protecting workplace safety. Labor unions help ensure that minimum standards are protected. But when nonunion companies can save money by endangering their workers, unionized companies find it hard to compete, and unions lose in the long run. If all companies must meet working standards that are strictly enforced, unions will have a level playing ground.

Labor lawyer Tom Geoghegan made the point that instead of fighting against free trade, the labor movement needs to focus on labor laws that protect union organizing. In that way, the labor movement would grow and thrive by creating new unionized workplaces instead of desperately holding on to their dying industrial and manufacturing strongholds.

As it stands, American workers who try to form a union regularly face losing their jobs. In his book *High-Tech Betrayal: Working and Organizing on the Shop Floor*, Victor Devinatz describes how he was fired from a high-tech medical manufacturing factory after he attempted to convince the minimum-wage workers to join a union. Such stories are rampant in America because union organizers have virtually no protection from being punished and fired by corporations that want to stop a union, and the situation is far worse in many Third World nations and dictatorships without the same traditions of an independent labor movement.

A study of the National Labor Relations Board found that between 1992 and 1997, employers fired or punished 125,000 workers in America for supporting a union, an enormous number that doesn't even include the workers who are too intimidated to file official complaints. A Human Rights Watch report concluded that the United States is violating international law by failing to protect its workers from retaliation by antiunion companies.

The Paycheck Protection Ploy

One of the conservatives' biggest efforts against labor is preventing unions from using their members' fees for political donations. "Paycheck protection" is the favorite Republican euphemism for destroying the unions' influence on our political system. The right wants the labor movement to be helpless in the face of huge corporate contributions to politicians, by prohibiting unions from spending dues on political expenditures, even though corporations already outspend labor by a 15-to-1 ratio.

Conservatives don't want to grant the same rights to shareholders of corporations. Although no one has ever proposed allowing shareholders to "opt out" of their corporation's spending on politics and lobbying, Republicans constantly encourage the "right" of union members to de-fund their unions' political activities.

If union members deserve "paycheck protection," then aren't shareholders entitled to the same protection for their money? After all, many shareholders don't like it when corporations spend their money to support political candidates and parties they oppose. Why shouldn't shareholders have the same rights as union members? It's true that shareholders can unite with other shareholders to elect leaders who won't spend their money on politics. But union members have the same right to chosen a new union or to disband the union entirely.

It's true that shareholders can choose to invest in a different company. Likewise, union members can choose to work at a different company or in a different industry. After all, most jobs in America are nonunion, whereas it's almost impossible nowadays to find a corporation to invest in that doesn't spend any money on lobbying or political candidates.

If the advocates of "paycheck protection" are truly concerned with the right of the individual not to be compelled to support certain political causes, then they should heartily endorse the notion of "dividend protection" for stockholders: if unions can't lobby without the permission of their members (and must offer a special payment to those who object), then shareholders should be entitled to special "political dividends" if they disagree with the lobbying of the corporations they own.

Since corporations are already have well-organized lobbying

and donation practices, conservatives assume that they can control the political process if workers are prohibited from similarly organizing to express their interests. "Paycheck protection" needs to be exposed as an attempt to expand the huge financial advantage that corporations hold over unions in the financing of elections.

The Global Union

Progressives must address globalization and its effect on labor rights. This doesn't mean that protectionism, the usual proposal of unions, is the answer. It's understandable that many workers and unions would like to see their jobs continue indefinitely. In a global economy, however, no American industry can be assured of permanent survival, so what progressives can work to ensure is a system of fair competition.

Union members respect picket lines because they understand that their own right to unionize would be threatened if others were denied their labor rights. Unions must hang together, or they will be broken separately. That principle needs to be extended around the world. Instead of seeking narrow protection for their own jobs, unions need to support the larger principle of protecting basic rights around the world.

It shouldn't be a progressive goal to eliminate jobs, even terrible jobs, in the underdeveloped world to preserve jobs in America. Instead, progressives must seek to improve these foreign jobs. Requiring human and labor rights to be obeyed around the world will not truly protect American labor. Because the labor cost of manufacturing most products in the Third World is so small, companies will continue to make shoes and other products overseas. These requirements will help raise the living standards of Third World workers with barely any increase in the cost of products to consumers. No one imagines that American labor standards can be imposed on the rest of the world. But some minimum standards can be upheld, such as bans on child labor, minimum wage and maximum hour rules, and health and safety regulations.

Americans are already losing jobs in the global economy, and all the protectionism in the world won't change that. Labor needs to stem the flow of jobs not by prohibiting it with trade barriers but by requiring these foreign jobs to be good jobs for workers around the world.. The labor movement needs to start organizing the new jobs being created in America: temps, service jobs, and high-tech jobs. Only then can unions rise again.

There are signs of hope. The success of the UPS strike shows how widely union activity is supported by the public when they're personally acquainted with the workers. It's only when unions are secretive and unknown that people start believing the prejudices against labor spread by the right.

There are signs of unions starting to enter new areas, even the elite service sector. In higher education, a growing number of graduate students and part-time instructors—often paid a tenth of regular faculty salaries at elite institutions to do the same teaching—are actively seeking union representation. When Berkeley's graduate instructors adopt a union by a 93 percent vote, as they did in the summer of 2000, it shows the potential popularity of union organizing.

Unions were a crucial part of raising living standards in America during the past century, and they continue to protect employees against the growing power of corporations. The rise of a new global capitalism means that unions must embrace the growing service sector of the economy in order to survive the shift of manufacturing around the world.

Instead of abandoning international organizations to the capitalists and urging a narrow protectionism by opposing free trade agreements (which makes unions look backward and purely self-interested), the labor movement needs to adopt a new approach. Unions must start demanding global institutions that will protect labor rights as human rights. Protecting labor rights around the world won't save all the jobs in America. But it will save the labor movement.

Chapter 14

THE RACE FOR JUSTICE

Defending Affirmative Action

Progressives have lost a lot of public support for affirmative action because they often end up arguing on the wrong terms. The key to winning an argument about affirmative action is to turn the subject to the deeper issue: racism.

All opposition to affirmative action stems from an implicit or explicit belief that racism doesn't really exist anymore. If there's not any racism, then affirmative action is, at best, some kind of dubious compensation for past discrimination, unfairness in the present to balance the unfairness of history. But if racism continues to exist, as we know it does, then affirmative action is a relatively small counterbalance against injustice. Proving the persistence of racism doesn't make affirmative action an open-and-shut case, but it does put it in a realistic perspective.

A defense of affirmative action must rest on today's racism, not that of the past. A successful argument also must be based on the idea of individual rights, not historical injustice. If you tell white people that affirmative action is necessary as compensation for slavery, it will typically cause a defensive reaction: I didn't have anything to do with slavery; my immigrant ancestors never had any slaves; why should I suffer because of that?

REPARATIONS

The campaign to provide reparations to African Americans for slavery, however well intentioned and even justified, often undermines the debate about affirmative action. It makes affirmative action seem like one component in reparations for past injustice, rather than a small factor fighting against current injustice. As a *Chicago Tribune* editorial put it, "What are set-asides and targets and outreach programs and all other such efforts if not reparations?" The answer is that affirmative action is a limited attempt to reach the ideal of equality, not a special preference for minorities. America isn't "already paying reparations"; it hasn't even met the basic requirement of equality compelled by the Fourteenth Amendment and the spirit of the Declaration of Independence.

The emphasis on reparations for slavery can be a tactical mistake precisely because the issue is so backward looking. The reparations argument can be more persuasive when it's made on the grounds that no compensation has ever been made to African Americans for slavery, Jim Crow laws, and the discrimination and segregation that have continued into the twenty-first century. Instead of a direct payment to African Americans, the "reparations" sought ought to be equality—equality in funding for schools, equality in the job market enforced by antidiscrimination laws, and equality in the legal system.

The demand for "reparations" falsely suggests that equality has been achieved and all we need to do is calculate the damage caused by past discrimination. Perhaps the debate over reparations should wait until after we have achieved true racial equality under the law, a goal that no one can reasonably oppose, but few people are willing to admit is far from being a reality.

Reparations were made by Congress to Japanese Americans whose families were imprisoned in camps on the West Coast during World War II, and it's not unreasonable to argue the same for African Americans. If the debate over reparations becomes an exploration of the inequality African Americans face, then it can accomplish a useful purpose. But if the reparations debate is perceived as a special handout for blacks, it will fail. The argument over reparations, like affirmative action, must ultimately turn on the persistence of racism.

Let's consider the plight of the unfortunate white male. As a white male, I have the firsthand experience of facing this oppression in the era of "reverse discrimination." It's terrible being a white man in America. Ninety-five percent of corporate CEOs and most of Congress and every single president in history look like me! The pressure is terrible! Those body image issues created by professional wrestlers—what real white man can live up to those standards? Belonging to the group that earns more money than anyone else—why, if you're not making $100,000 a year by age thirty-five, you feel inadequate. All these people claiming they should get the privileges of white men don't understand how tough it is—without our special privileges, how could white men run the world? Surely we don't want to burden women and minorities with the difficult task of controlling all the legislative bodies and major corporations in the United States.

Dan Quayle is a perfect example of how affirmative action works. Here's a guy without great intelligence or special talents who evades the draft and gets into law school because of his wealthy family—and he becomes a U.S. senator and vice-president of the United States. Despite all the jokes about Quayle, the planet did not melt down during his watch. If mediocre white guys can do an adequate job without being well qualified, why not give the mediocre nonwhite guys (and women) a chance? Who knows, maybe once we've truly integrated our corporations and our schools and our legislatures, we'll be able to adopt a system of pure merit. Until then, maintaining the status quo of affirmative action for white men is intolerable, and affirmative action programs to help women and minorities have been the only effective solution offered.

Conservatives argue that racism doesn't exist in any important sense because the Civil Rights Act banned it in 1965. But the evidence proves otherwise. What about all the blacks who face discrimination in hiring? What about the innocent blacks harassed and arrested and even imprisoned because of racial profiling and bias in our legal system? What about the blacks who must attend substandard, underfunded public schools while whites send their kids to the area's best public schools in the suburbs? What about the well-established segregation and housing discrimination? What about the difficulty many blacks have getting loans? What about the indignity of having trouble getting a cab or being treated as a criminal in a store? What is all that if not "second-class" status? What is all that if not racism?

Affirmative action measures are merely a partial solution to the continuing problems of racism and sexism. Set-asides are necessary to provide equal opportunity for women and minorities who are excluded from the political connections that are often needed to obtain contracts. Targets are necessary to prevent the widespread race and sex discrimination that prevails without affirmative action. Small preferences in college admissions are necessary to provide access to the top colleges in a country where minorities, on average, are systematically placed in inferior public schools compared with those attended by whites.

The point to remember about affirmative action is that it has always existed, and unfortunately, no one is proposing to abolish it. The only issue in the current debate is whether affirmative action for women and minorities might be eliminated. The age-old affirmative action programs for wealthy white men and their offspring will persist unabated. Affirmative action for white men doesn't have a name—it doesn't register on the radar screens of mainstream media debates on the topic.

Affirmative action needs to be divided into two general categories—higher education and job opportunities—because the arguments defending them are different, though equally strong.

Affirmative action in education is crucial because everyone deserves an opportunity to learn. A minimally qualified student who receives a small preference over a slightly more qualified student to gain admission to college isn't hurting anyone. No one worries that "less qualified" students are endangering the public or performing incompetently at a job if they get a college education. Students ought to have access to the same quality of education in a public school, no matter what their race or class. In today's economy, a college education is not some rare accomplishment; it's essential that everyone have a chance to attend college.

Why is it good for African American students to attend elite universities? First of all, the students at these top universities are more likely to graduate than the students at other universities are. The graduation rate for blacks ranges from around 76 percent at MIT to 50 percent at Berkeley to 30 percent at San Jose State. Overall, only around one-third of blacks finish college, about 25 percentage points behind whites. The principal reason that blacks—and other students—fail to graduate is not affirmative action but money.

Affirmative action is essential because these elite institutions are stepping-stones to power. Networking with the children of the elite, not to mention using the prestigious reputation of an elite degree, is important to future advancement. The elite colleges have some of the largest resources to devote to education. With the biggest libraries and best-paid professors in small classes, the opportunity for quality education is usually better than at a less prestigious college.

Elite universities, despite a symbolic attachment to affirmative action, still don't admit African Americans or Latinos anywhere in proportion to the college-age population. A white student today is far more likely to be admitted to a top college than is an African American or Latino student, despite all the attention given to affirmative action. Clearly, the opportunities for whites are better than for minorities despite affirmative action programs.

Conservatives want to eliminate the tiny amount of affirmative action exercised at elite American colleges (most black college students never receive any assistance in admissions) but never say a word about the fact that far more whites than blacks receive special preferences to gain admission to these elite institutions, most notably those for athletes and alumni.

Affirmative Hiring

Affirmative action is necessary not as compensation for past injustices but in order to counteract the racial preferences for whites. Affirmative action helps prevent discrimination in hiring. Discrimination against hiring blacks is widespread, but antidiscrimination laws do little to prevent it. Typically, antidiscrimination lawsuits are filed only by professionals who are fired or not promoted because of race or sex (most complaints are made by women, not minorities). The far more common discrimination against poor blacks seeking entry-level jobs is almost never detected, because these job seekers lack the resources to sue and discrimination in hiring is almost impossible to prove. One study of identically qualified whites and blacks who applied for entry-level service jobs found that the whites were 55 percent more likely than blacks to be offered a job. Imagine how much worse the discrimination against blacks would be without any affirmative action, without any of this pressure to ensure equality.

When it comes to employment, quotas are justified in many circumstances. If an employer or an industry has a long history of discrimination, simply encouraging diversity will never be enough. The only way to force equality is to impose a quota, or a set-aside, until the discrimination ends.

Only a tiny number of minority workers actually obtain jobs because of quotas, mostly in a few government jobs or certain government-financed construction work. Vast sectors of the economy have no quotas for minorities and women whatsoever—affirmative action is more often a slogan than an actual policy. As a result, employment discrimination in America is still rampant.

Nonetheless, it can be difficult to convince many people to support quotas. A better option for progressives is to urge stronger enforcement of antidiscrimination laws, including random checks of businesses and government agencies using equally qualified testers of various races.

Fighting White Supremacy

Every argument for affirmative action must stand on the reality of white supremacy today. This doesn't mean you should necessarily use the phrase "white supremacy," because it's easily misunderstood by a lot of whites. But white people must always be reminded that racism didn't end with Abraham Lincoln or Martin Luther King Jr., that it continues to infect our society today. Affirmative action is not compensation for the injustices that occurred two hundred years ago but those of two minutes ago.

Given the delusion that all people of any race have equal opportunities to pursue the American dream, the opposition to affirmative action is understandable. If I believed that equality existed and affirmative action merely compensated for past harms that I had no part in committing, I'd probably oppose it, too.

The Republican assault on affirmative action might be more morally persuasive if conservatives had any intention of eliminating discrimination in housing, stopping job bias, bringing equal financing to schools, or ending poverty and its differential impact on minorities. Far from ending racial discrimination, the right has fought efforts to end racism and sexism.

It is important to maintain the difference between "affirmative action" and "racial preferences," not just for the sake of rhetorical advantage, but also to be accurate. Racial preferences exist throughout America, almost always to the disadvantage of minorities. Affirmative action is a small subcategory of racial preferences that attempts to offset a few of the disadvantages created by racial preferences for well-off whites.

As a white person, I oppose racial preferences. I cannot tolerate the idea that certain people get advantages simply because of the color of their skin and the geography of their ancestry. That's why we need to expand affirmative action in order to end these racial preferences for whites.

Should racial preferences be eliminated? Absolutely. Should affirmative action be eliminated? Not unless and until all other racial preferences are gone. The well-established bias against women and minorities before affirmative action (and continuing despite its presence) shows that a world without affirmative action is not a level playing field. The primary flaw in affirmative action in America is that it does too little, rather than too much, to help racial minorities. Even with affirmative action, blacks and Latinos face incredible amounts of discrimination from entry-level jobs to corporate boardrooms.

A few opponents of affirmative action are willing to admit the extent of racism in America. But, they argue, affirmative action only makes things worse by stigmatizing minorities. Is the white male who resents seeing a black person promoted over him suddenly going to accept this if affirmative action is abolished? Much of the resentment of affirmative action is simple racism, and abolishing affirmative action won't cure that disease. In a racist and sexist society, successful blacks and Latinos and women always face resentment. Affirmative action didn't create racial resentment; in fact, the level of interpersonal bias has declined owing to affirmative action because most whites in direct contact with minorities at the workplace learn how to deal with diversity.

Even if affirmative action caused some white resentment, that wouldn't be an adequate argument against it. Social justice always causes anger. Many whites were angry when slavery was abolished or segregated bathrooms were prohibited or the army was integrated or discrimination in housing and jobs was banned. When we let racists dictate our public policy as a justification for banning affirmative action, we only encourage bigotry.

For progressives, the key to winning the affirmative action debate is to make people understand that racial profiling exists throughout American society. Most people think it's absolutely wrong for police to target minorities, based merely on their race, for searches. The "crime" of "driving while black" is symbolic of the larger crime of "living while black" that African Americans must struggle against. Everyone from security guards to cab drivers to passersby assumes that blacks, especially young black men, are potential criminals. From housing to schools to jobs, women and minorities face tremendous barriers to success from racial and gender preferences that benefit white males.

WHY PROGRESSIVES MUST PAY ATTENTION TO RACE

It has become common for white, middle-aged progressives to argue that the left has failed in America because it has splintered into "special interest" groups that focus on race, gender, or sexual orientation. According to this analysis, progressives need to focus on class above all else and pursue "universal" programs that will appeal to the white political mainstream.

Ralph Nader's campaign was an example of how progressive movements can fall short of their potential when they don't specifically target people of color, women, and gays and lesbians. Nader was virtually the perfect progressive on nearly every issue—but because of his failure to attract a diverse following, he couldn't establish a genuine mass movement in the 2000 elections.

Conservatives can afford to ignore feminists and minorities because by doing so, they sacrifice only a tiny number of votes. For progressives, though, a straight white male movement is doomed to failure. Among the potential progressive voters, white males are a small minority, and failing to reach out to other groups will doom the left to continued irrelevance.

The pundits in both parties traditionally have believed that talking about racial justice, gender equity, and equality under the law, regardless of sexual orientation, is certain to be a losing strategy. Anyone who endorses these positions strongly, they think, will lose the support of the white guys whom they consider to be the swing voters determining the outcome of elections.

Progressives have, however, changed the nature of campaigns. Outright racism and sexism and even homophobia have become

---

unacceptable in American political life. The white swing voters no longer run scared from race and gender. The fact that George W. Bush had to condemn Bob Jones University's racist policies and strongly endorsed the appearance of diversity at the 2000 Republican National Convention showed the change in the swing voters. In the past, many politicians felt that they couldn't endorse equality without alienating voters; now the opposite is true.

For African Americans and other disempowered groups, challenging the political status quo is a riskier scheme than it is for disillusioned white progressives. Minority groups need a compelling reason to support progressive candidates and progressive ideas. Whereas conservative Democrats can appeal to "the lesser of two evils," progressives must provide genuine reasons for support.

Racism, sexism, and homophobia are too powerful and too important to leave for special-interest groups to solve with only tacit support from the white guys. If white male progressives are uncomfortable talking about these issues, they should realize that everyone else is uncomfortable watching them ignore these issues.

Many progressives have become disillusioned with affirmative action because it has failed to improve the lives of most women and minorities. A few middle-class blacks may benefit from access to elite institutions, but the poor rarely gain much.

The answer to these shortcomings is not to end affirmative action but to expand the concept and its impact. Having more black MBAs and lawyers may seem like a wasted effort if you regard MBAs and lawyers as worthless leeches on society. But more women and minorities in positions of power—aside from being beneficial to society as a whole—can create role models for the future and help mitigate racist and sexist attitudes.

Some progressives have argued for ending race-based affirmative action (which often benefits less disadvantaged middle-class minorities) and replacing it with class-based affirmative action. Exclusively class-based affirmative action is problematic because it denies the existence of racism. According to class-based reasoning, African Americans are disadvantaged only insofar as they are poor. But discrimination in America is more than wallet deep. Poor blacks are more likely than poor whites to live in ghettos with extreme poverty, to attend inferior schools, and to be exposed to high crime rates. The rare middle-class black student who goes to a quality school in a mostly white area may not be treated the same as white students and is more likely to be kept away from advanced-level, college-track classes. Even if such blacks do manage to beat the odds and graduate with a college degree, they face racial profiling from police, social discrimination, housing discrimination, and job discrimination.

Instead of abandoning affirmative action, progressives need to reconceive and expand it. There is no contradiction between race-based and class-based affirmative action; to the contrary, they reinforce each other and strengthen the pursuit of equality in America. Just as defending race-based affirmative action requires revealing the truth about racial discrimination in America, class-based affirmative action requires progressives to point out the prevalence of class discrimination in this country. Ultimately, the success of affirmative action depends on whether or not progressives can appeal to the American commitment to equality by pointing out how far the reality of inequality diverges from our ideals.

Chapter 15

UNIVERSAL HEALTH CARE

The problem with American health care is not that we spend too little money but that we spend it unwisely. We throw huge amounts of money into emergency care and very little into preventive care. We refuse to provide basic medical coverage for everyone, but we pay huge amounts giving universal health care for very sick people. With 40 million Americans lacking health insurance and many more underinsured, the crisis in health care cannot be ignored.

Health care is a question of paying now or paying later. An organized system of universal health care, if properly designed, isn't more expensive than our current disorganized system of universal health care, in which treatment is delayed.

If the government paid for every American to receive biannual medical checkups, the cost would be large—but imagine the benefits of diseases caught at an early stage when they are more treatable; a longer life span in which healthier Americans spent more time working, which would increase productivity and tax revenues; and fewer emergency room visits from people who too poor to see a doctor anywhere else.

Locking the emergency room door and letting the poor die on the street is appalling. As a result, we already have a "welfare" system; it's simply a grossly inefficient system that treats people at the most expensive level of medicine. Instead of taking a sick child to see the doctor, the poor parent takes her to the emergency room, sometimes waiting until the child is very sick. The cost to everyone, and the harm to the child, is much greater.

Health care reform requires that we understand that medical care is an investment that produces beneficial results over the long term. Healthier children do better in school. Healthier adults are more productive at work and find it easier to get and keep a job—and thereby generate more tax revenue.

The initial "cost" of universal health care may seem substantial, but it reaps enormous benefits in lower emergency care costs, increased productivity, and long-term health. Winning the argument about health care requires discussing something that policy wonks never do: the value of a human life. If people could have lived years and sometimes decades longer with an intelligent health care system, the benefit to society would be enormous, even if it weren't always a bonus when measured in narrow economic terms.

The biggest flaw in the Clinton health care plan was its design to appease special interests by rejecting a single-payer system. The special interests opposed it anyway, giving us Harry and Louise's paranoid babbling on TV commercials ("Universal health care? That sounds like Communism to me!"). The efficiency of a single-payer system was thus replaced by a proposed cumbersome government bureaucracy that could easily be attacked by all sides.

When the Clinton administration floated the idea of universal health care, conservatives tried to stop it by claiming that the plan would prevent Americans from choosing their doctors and would lead to rationing. Ironically, every evil imagined about universal health care ended up becoming a reality under private managed care. HMOs and the "free market" didn't liberate Americans; instead, people lost their freedom and control over their medical care.

The fear that universal health care might lead to rationing was wildly overblown. We already have rationing in regard to organ transplants, and no one objects to this. The real danger is that certain expensive operations are not treated like organ transplants, and ability to pay rather than medical need becomes the overriding factor. No one ever imagines that rich people will be denied an operation or treatment if it's available and they have the money to pay for it. But if it is a choice between a rich person or a poor person dying for lack of resources, no one believes that money should determine life-and-death medical decisions. In the end, HMOs imposed a rationing system of this kind.

It's quite possible that HMOs can cut costs more than a government system can. That's why legislation was passed to regulate HMOs and prevent them from "cutting costs" by refusing to allow medical procedures that doctors, but not corporations, think are necessary. It's the rest of society that must pay these costs. If someone develops serious health problems and has to quit working or, after retirement, gets ill from a long-term problem, the HMO doesn't have to pay anything for the illness that might have been prevented with adequate medical care. It's the individual, or the hospital, or the taxpayers who have to pick up the tab while the HMOs pick up the profits.

Conservatives are never afraid to pass tax cuts they can't pay for, because they have faith that the economy will grow to compensate for these losses. Progressives need to make the same argument for health care: no matter what the alleged cost of universal health care, the long-term benefits of a healthier population will outweigh it. Unfortunately, a narrow cost-benefit analysis can't take into account all the social and economic benefits of people living longer and paying taxes.

From an economic standpoint, the huge investment we make raising and educating children—usually exceeding several hundred thousand dollars in government subsidies alone, and much more in private money—will be lost prematurely if these individuals die before retirement, as many Americans do. Even after the age of retirement, these seniors have enormous value as family, friends, volunteers, and workers, especially as we move from an industrial to a technological economy and the number of people working into their seventies, eighties, and nineties increases.

Universal health care can be justified solely on the grounds of creating longer, happier lives for people. Good health is also one of most important factors for economic productivity. Our future economic health makes universal health care as beneficial as universal schooling.

Chapter 16

GREENER POLITICS

Progressives and the Environment

The environment is probably the most popular progressive program of all. Many people who don't otherwise care about leftist politics support saving the environment. And the future is bright: the extent of environmental awareness and support among children is far greater than that of any other public policy.

Left-wing cynics might argue that environmentalism is popular because it employs the "fuzzy animal" approach—show anyone pandas or penguins, proclaim them threatened, and the cooing of concern is inevitable. The same is true to a lesser degree of the pristine national parks or impressive redwoods. Sometimes it seems that the only way to get privileged Americans to care about poor people around the world is to paint adorable stripes on them or install an awe-inspiring fountain to spray out of their mouths.

The left needs to use the popular appeal of environmentalism. The environment is an unusual issue for progressives because the public doesn't need much convincing to accept its basic goodness. Instead, the left needs to challenge people to go beyond feel-good environmentalism.

Some environmental issues are easy to win in the public mind (although it's much harder to overcome corporate power in the halls of Congress). Few people are willing to support dirty air and dirty water. But other environmental issues can be more difficult to win. Too often, the left gets trapped between banana slugs and jobs, choosing spotted owls or logs.

ANIMAL RIGHTS AND THE HAZARDS OF PUBLICITY

The left is accustomed to being confrontational because that's the only way to grab public attention for little-noticed issues. People for the Ethical Treatment of Animals (PETA) is legendary for its publicity-grabbing techniques on behalf of animal rights.

PETA offends many people partly because they confront very personal things. Nobody likes to be told that his lunch is immoral. PETA also unnecessarily alienates a lot of people who might otherwise agree with their goals.

When PETA objects to the Green Bay Packers' name (because it's a reference to meatpacking), their credibility is diminished. After all, the Packers don't have a blood-dripping mascot or reenact animal slaughter during their halftime show. No one associates the team with meat, and it's difficult to imagine that a substantial number of vegetarian football fans would regard the nickname as a personal insult in the way that many Native Americans look on the demeaning names and mascots used by sports teams.

The slogan "rights for rats" (to use an example of the PETA attack on the TV show *Survivor*) is probably not the best way to convert people to the idea of treating animals humanely. Most folks regard rats as vermin to get rid of, not intelligent creatures with rights equivalent to those for human beings. The prejudice against rats may be unfortunate, but it's essential to recognize how powerful it is before engaging in protests. Most people aren't likely to oppose eating rats when they're willing to poison them.

If properly approached, even a corned beef sandwich–chomping carnivore can recognize that vegetarianism is a better lifestyle. It's better for public health, better for the planet, and certainly better for the unfortunate sandwich fodder, which lives a nasty, brutish existence before being taken away for slaughter. Nobody ought to support the unnecessary killing of animals for corporate research. But instead of engaging in the difficult work of bringing public attention to these facts, PETA always goes for the cheap publicity stunt. More people now certainly recognize PETA's name; the problem is that no one takes the group or their issues seriously.

When environmentalists can focus on the massive public subsidies provided by the government to corporations that devastate the environment, the argument is simple. Should the government (or, to make it more personal, "your tax dollars") subsidize the already enormous profits of big corporations by building free logging roads exclusively to assist their deforestation? Should the government pay to turn forests into wasteland by selling the logging rights at below-market prices?

Choosing between nature and jobs presents a dilemma for most people. Forcing a choice between nature and public handouts to corporations is an argument that's much easier to win.

When environmentalism hits people in the pocketbook, even someone strongly committed to saving the planet may begin to waver. On issues such as recycling, pollution, and global warming, the public is recognizing that the long-term cost of environmental damage is far greater than the short-term cost of sensible environmental policies.

Genetic Engineering

One of the most contentious environmental issues at the moment deals with genetically engineered (GE) food. Unfortunately, both sides have been guilty of bad science: the activists who oppose GE often leave people with the impression that vengeful mutant vegetables will soon be stalking humans, while the GE companies and their scientists refuse to acknowledge any of the dangers posed by this unique technology. The winner in the public debate will not be the one that provides the greatest exaggerations of the dangers or the benefits of GE, but the side that can offer the most reasonable position that protects public health while enabling scientific advances.

The advocates of genetic engineering argue that this new science is no different from the crossbreeding that farmers have done for centuries to create new, better varieties. But there is a difference. Crossbreeding requires experimenters to work within certain known biological limits, whereas genetic engineering removes these limits, enabling scientists to create entirely new organisms. Putting a salmon gene in a tomato or a bacterium gene in corn allows biological change on a pace and a scale unknown and untested in history.

Until activists raised an uproar about GE products, anyone creating genetically engineered organisms and selling food made from them didn't even need to inform the Food and Drug Administration or to do any testing before putting their unlabeled products on supermarket shelves. The companies seeking FDA approval still don't need to do extensive tests on health effects or environmental impact.

It took a private consumer group to reveal in 2000 that genetically engineered animal feed corn that hadn't been approved for human consumption was present in foods such as tortillas, taco shells, and breakfast cereal around the country. When an untested science is foisted on the public without its knowledge, the dangers can be severe.

Recent research discovered that monarch butterfly larvae could be killed by the pollen of genetically engineered corn, an example of the unexpected effects of this new science. Further scientific studies suggest that the monarch butterfly probably won't be threatened by this technology, but the point is that none of this testing was done until after most U.S. farmers had converted to genetically engineered seeds.

It's true that no genetically engineered product sold in America has been proved to be harmful. But when we're dealing with the world's food supply, the precautionary principle needs to be considered. In the 1980s, no one in England imagined that it might be dangerous to feed sheep's brains to cows in order to increase profits with cheap protein. The result was mad cow disease, which killed dozens of people (and may kill many more) and required virtually all the cattle in England to be killed. Even though the U.S. government claims there has never been a case of mad cow disease in America, just to be safe, techniques such as feeding sheep's brains to animals are prohibited. After the terrifying experience with mad cow disease, Europeans are correct to distrust untested food technology.

It's possible that genetic engineering could greatly benefit the world by increasing agricultural production. It's also possible that the misuse of genetic engineering could create a superbug (resistant to the antipest bacteria used by organic farmers and incorporated into many GE plants) or a superweed (which would crossbreed with the GE plants and be virtually immune to pesticides) or have some devastating and unexpected effect. The rapid and largely untested dominance of GE crops in the United States (about half of the soybeans and a third of the corn) would have an enormous impact on the world's food supply if anything went wrong.

Requiring better safety regulations and labeling for genetic engineering won't suddenly bring the world to the brink of starvation. There is plenty of food to feed the world. The cause of world hunger is political, not technological. The problems are world poverty and war, not farming techniques. Foisting expensive bioengineered seeds onto the rest of the world won't solve this fundamental source of hunger.

Although there isn't strong public support for a total ban on genetic engineering, most people want to know what they're eating and feel confident that adequate testing has been done. If the law requires consumers to be informed that their orange juice is made from concentrate, why shouldn't they be informed that their food contains genetically engineered products?

The issue of labeling sparked an internal debate among activists, many of whom saw labeling as a waste of time. What they really wanted was a ban on GE food, not just an inoffensive label informing people that their food contained it.

But labeling is a winning issue with strong public support. No one can easily oppose providing more information to consumers. Once the public understands how many of their foods use GE ingredients, the likely reaction will be widespread demands to make sure of adequate testing and controls.

As with other environmental issues, genetic engineering is a topic on which environmentalists can pressure the public to adopt a green approach, but only if they resist the extremist arguments. Alarmist slogans may bring temporary support, but over the long run, environmentalists need to seek compromises. Pragmatic environmentalism doesn't mean that environmental groups should always support the Democratic Party even when it's failing to protect the environment. Instead, environmentalists need to be pragmatic by focusing on issues that are winnable and have broad public support.

Chapter 17

WHY WE NEED WELFARE AND HOW TO CHANGE IT

Welfare is the most demonized issue of our times. The reason is that American politics operates by a simple selfish rule: when government helps you, it's working; when government helps somebody else, it's welfare. Except during a recession, very few people regard welfare as essential to their lives. In order for welfare to succeed in the minds of the public, progressives must both criticize the current system and advocate the extension of welfare to more effective policies.

To a certain extent, progressives need to stand up and defend the value of welfare. Welfare programs have a remarkable track record of success for a huge number of people. Medicare, Medicaid, Social Security, unemployment insurance, food stamps, and Aid to Families with Dependent Children all have had a dramatic effect on alleviating poverty, reducing death rates, and helping the poor. The programs targeted at the poor—AFDC, Medicaid, food stamps—have been far more efficient than the middle-class entitlement programs that politicians regard as sacrosanct. The social benefits of welfare have been enormous.

Progressives must also realize the shortcomings of welfare. Welfare is not a progressive policy; it's a liberal policy that progressives have accepted as a political compromise. Liberals want welfare because it's a remarkably inexpensive way of dealing with the poverty created in an unequal capitalist system. The liberal welfare state, however, is far from a progressive ideal because it doesn't offer permanent solutions to the problems of poverty.

Everybody hates welfare. Even people on welfare hate welfare. That's why a progressive solution can't defend the status quo.

Neoliberals want to offer smaller welfare handouts and preserve the basic inequality of the "free market" system. Progressives want to eliminate the need for welfare programs by establishing a living minimum wage, equal schools, quality day-care programs, and a public works project for people who fall through the cracks.

Progressives made the mistake of viewing "workfare" as a purely punitive approach ("no work, no food") when they should have attacked workfare for failing to go far enough and failing to provide real jobs for people who need them. Neoliberals who believe in "free market" fantasies such as a "natural unemployment rate" (or the inevitable link between higher wages and reduced economic growth) cannot conceive of genuinely progressive ideas for government jobs programs.

When welfare programs failed, it was because they were designed to do so. Large, segregated public housing projects created enormous ghettos of poverty because liberals refused to fight a political battle to help the poor find housing in all neighborhoods, regardless of race or class. (The current move toward housing "vouchers" is simply a way to let the "free market" continue the same disastrous economic and racial segregation that the housing projects established.) If a racist and incompetently run housing program or school system fails, progressives shouldn't rush to defend it. They should, however, counter the delusion that the "free market" (which helped cause the problem) offers the only solution to it. When progressives are caught in the neoliberal trap of choosing between a failed government program and a "free market" solution that will make matters worse, they always lose the argument.

In essence, the right wants to privatize poverty: let the churches and social groups handle the poor, and keep government away. Even more than most privatization policies, this one is doomed to failure because there isn't enough private charity devoted to helping the poor handle all the problems caused by poverty. In fact, the success of private charities at helping the poor is made possible by the government's welfare programs. If these private charities had to meet the basic housing and food needs of all poor people, they would quickly be overwhelmed.

Progressives can win only if they keep offering alternatives rather than merely defending the status quo. Given the choice between dangerous housing projects versus privatized vouchers or inferior public schools versus privatized vouchers, most people will support the idea of trying something new. But if progressives can change the terms of the debate and introduce ideas such as equal financing and innovative desegregation options into a tired debate about vouchers, the left can revitalize these arguments in new directions.

Progressives want to end welfare, but they don't want to end it by punishing the poor and offering no solutions. The left wants to end welfare by creating a just economic system in which all Americans have an opportunity to succeed.

ENDING CLASS WARFARE

It's common to hear conservatives describe progressive proposals as promoting "class warfare" or "class envy." Class envy, though, is perfectly normal. Poor people in urban areas whose children attend lousy schools should envy the rich suburban public schools where there's plenty of funding for swimming pools and small classes and advanced placement courses. Poor people struggling on welfare should envy the large corporations that receive huge handouts from the government. The working poor should envy all those rich people who pay a smaller proportion of their income in payroll and sales taxes and who get a special tax break on capital gains taxes for their investments. The poor who spend so much of their income on rent because affordable housing isn't available should envy the millionaires who deduct the mortgage payments on their multimillion dollar mansions from their taxes.

The message isn't "screw the rich"; it's "stop screwing the poor." Progressives aren't trying to start a class war; the left is trying to end the ongoing class war of the government's favoring the rich, a class war in which the poor people are the casualties and the rich are profiting. Progressives want to end class conflict by creating a greater equality of opportunities. Progressives aren't arguing for the confiscation of money from the wealthy (Donald Trump was the only political candidate to propose that). Progressives are simply arguing for equality: equal funding for public schools, equal job and educational opportunities, equal taxation, equal financing of welfare for the poor compared with what the government sets aside for corporate welfare.

Talking about inequality and poverty and tax breaks isn't "class warfare." Warfare requires casualties: lives lost and people injured.

Class warfare is what happens to all the people who die prematurely because the lack of health insurance deprives them of needed health care. Class warfare is what happens to the thousands of employees who are maimed or killed on the job every year because of inadequate safety regulation. Class warfare is what happens to the hundreds of thousands of Americans harmed every year by pollution because corporations use their money to keep environmental protections weak. Class warfare is what happens to the thousands of primarily poor, nonwhites killed every year owing to the proliferation of guns in America.

The wealthy don't suffer in any class war; the poor do. Class envy and class warfare will disappear only when America lives up to its billing as the land of opportunity for all.

The greatest problem with the "welfare state" was that it relied on a Band-Aid approach to social problems rather than a public investment approach. It's like having construction workers fill in potholes in a road every day because it's cheaper—in the short run—than repaving the whole road and having it work well. The potholes are a nuisance; the construction workers are an impediment to everyone making progress down the road; and it's a waste of time and money to put skilled workers at the task of endlessly filling up broken roads.

Fortunately, we don't have this problem when it comes to our roads. We invest huge amounts of government money to provide nice roads for everyone—far more money than we spend on welfare. If we're willing to spend so much to make good highways, why won't we invest as much money in the lives of our neighbors? Since everyone agrees that roads in the most need of repair require the largest public investments, why should we object to having our money used to help those people who need help the most?

The answer is that most Americans don't object to this at all. But they've become convinced that the "welfare state" amounts to nothing more than filling in potholes rather than solving problems. Most clever of all, conservatives have managed to push the idea that filling in potholes creates the problem of bad roads. The notion is absurd: it should be clear to everyone that poverty, not an antipoverty program, is the cause of social problems. Instead of cursing the potholes and blaming the construction workers, progressives need to offer a way of fixing the system that creates these problems.

The problem with the safety net is that it's money wasted on a failure in the system. Helping people get a decent job is obviously superior to helping them out when they can't find a job. The metaphor of the "safety net" needs to be replaced with a "safety harness"—preventing people from falling, rather than simply assisting them at a minimal level after they fall. A "safety harness" is more efficient than a safety net, and it enables the poor to lift themselves up—the favorite metaphor of conservatives.

Unfortunately, corporate America is usually opposed to most of the measures needed to provide a "safety harness"—government-provided child care, adequate education and training, and government work programs. Even though it would obviously be better for the country if we paid people to improve our communities rather than simply handing out welfare, the idea of full employment is anathema to the business community, which depends on the unemployed and the underemployed to keep wages low.

The problem with "workfare" is that it's too often punitive rather than productive. Instead of giving real jobs to people on welfare and providing education, child care, health care, and other needed programs, the "workfare" approach simply tries to save money by punishing welfare recipients and kicking them out of the program if they don't jump through the right hoops.

While progressives shouldn't defend welfare, they should refute the silly idea that welfare causes poverty. The real causes of poverty can easily be found in unemployment, the growing inequality of income, and the lack of economic and educational opportunities in impoverished areas.

The logical fallacy here is confusing a cure with a treatment. Welfare has never been a cure for poverty. Nor does welfare cause poverty. Welfare treats the victims of poverty. When poverty increases, as it did in America during the 1980s, there will be more people to treat. As it turns out, the "welfare causes poverty" nonsense is directly refuted by the economic facts: when welfare programs were severely cut during the past two decades, poverty and the need for welfare increased.

Welfare is not caused by laziness. Of course, there are lazy people, and some of them live off welfare (if you call that living), some of them work in your office (you know who they are), some of them play golf all day while making money from low-taxed capital gains. But welfare doesn't make people lazy. If you want to get rich, having kids on welfare is the worst possible way to gain wealth. Not one millionaire has ever recommended welfare as the path to fabulous riches.

This doesn't mean our current welfare system works. It does mean that progressives need to offer alternatives to the welfare state rather than simply opposing the punitive "reforms" supported by the Democrats and the Republicans.

Most of the solutions to the welfare system don't involve changing welfare itself. At a fundamental level, giving money to poor families for basic survival needs is not a system that can be easily changed without dooming children to a life of hunger, homelessness, and despair (as proposals to cut off welfare after a few years do). The best welfare reform involves changing the economic situation that creates poverty for millions of Americans. This means raising the minimum wage (instead of cutting welfare payments) and creating universal health insurance to increase the incentive for the poor to seek work rather than charity. New job programs and improved educational opportunities from preschool to college are necessary for transforming the welfare state.

Chapter 18

ENDING CORPORATE WELFARE
AS WE KNOW IT

The real welfare queens in America wear dark suits and silk ties. They are undertaxed CEOs, not unwed mothers. They line up their lobbyists in congressional offices instead of lining up at a social service agency. They own the media instead of being demonized by them.

Corporate welfare permeates American society. A *Time* magazine investigation in 1998 noted: "The Federal Government alone shells out $125 billion a year in corporate welfare." Yet this enormous benefit for the wealthiest in America receives far less attention and criticism than do the much smaller welfare programs that assist the poorest people. No president has ever promised to "end corporate welfare as we know it." To do so would threaten the lifeline of campaign money that corporations provide to candidates.

Despite its size and importance, corporate welfare often falls below the media's radar screen. Subsidies, protectionism, and obscure tax breaks aren't considered sexy stories. Business news glorifies corporate welfare rather than critically examining it. Politicians take credit for "creating" jobs in their districts by winning the bribery wars that benefit companies. Lobbyists target enormous resources to benefits for specific companies and industries, but because the cost of corporate welfare is spread across all taxpayers, there is no powerful constituency demanding the end of these wasteful giveaways.

The best thing about attacking corporate welfare is that everybody's against it. No idea is so widely supported in Washington and so widely opposed in the rest of the country as the belief that corporations should receive subsidies, protections, and giveaways from government.

THE $500 PLAN

One problem with launching a successful campaign attacking corporate welfare is that most Americans feel that the government would waste the money no matter how it was spent. Imagine that progressives supported huge tax cuts by sharply reducing corporate welfare: $500 for every single American every single year if a substantial part of corporate welfare could be eliminated, whether in the form of tax breaks or government gifts. If you're a taxpayer, you get $500 directly. If you're on welfare, the $500 goes to provide job training and child care. If you're a child, the money is sent directly to your school for increasing education spending. A plan to give every American $5,000 over the next ten years (that's $20,000 for a family of four) beats anything the Republicans or the Democrats can offer.

Is it feasible? With 280 million Americans, that's about $140 billion to trim from corporate welfare—a large task but not an

(continued)

impossible one. An independent agency could monitor corporate welfare spending and return the "rebate" figure for each American every year. If $70 billion were cut, then the individual rebate would be $250. If it were only $14 billion, then $50 would be returned. This would put permanent pressure on Congress and the White House to cut corporate welfare spending and give the direct benefits of doing so back to the American people.

Of course, the $500 plan isn't perfect from a progressive perspective. Bill Gates would get as much money as a homeless person would. A rich kid's school would receive as much as would a poor kid in a school that's falling apart. But $500 plan isn't meant to solve every problem. Tax reform and educational equity need to be pursued aggressively on their own to help the poor. The $500 plan does, however, create a clear benefit to ending corporate welfare and make a dramatic statement about how much money is at stake.

Welfare for the poor can inspire genuine debates about whether a social safety net is needed. Abortion or taxes or schools or capital punishment can quickly divide any political discussion. But corporate welfare has no public defender—there are only secret supporters, who fasten hidden riders onto massive appropriations bills.

For progressives, virtually every issue can be part of an attack on corporate welfare. Gun control? It's about gun makers who want easy profits without having to pay for the cost of the damage and deaths they cause. Environmental regulations? It's about polluting companies that want corporate welfare by being able to pollute the environment for free. Capital gains tax breaks? It's a lower tax rate for investments in corporations than for other forms of income.

Corporate welfare is also the easy solution when progressives are asked how they will pay for new or expanded programs. How can we afford more money for schools? Cut corporate welfare. How can we afford universal health care? Cut corporate welfare. How can we lower taxes on the poor? Cut corporate welfare.

Another advantage of attacking corporate welfare is that it's a way to form an alliance with many conservatives. To genuine conservatives, corporate welfare is a violation of everything the free market stands for. Corporate welfare is the biggest part of the "big government" that conservatives constantly rail against. Corporate welfare distorts the free market. It creates a dangerous dependency on government handouts. It rewards inefficiency and forces companies to waste money in the pursuit of public bribery.

To genuine liberals, corporate welfare is the worst example of how the federal government helps the rich while ignoring the poor. Most people assume that the rich pay for the programs to help the poor. But the extent of corporate welfare proves the opposite: it's the working poor and the middle class who pay large tax bills in order to help the rich.

Corporate welfare has always been with us, but its power and influence have risen sharply in recent years. As elections increasingly depend on money, corporations are learning to tie their donations to preferential treatment in tax breaks, deregulation, and government funding. The economic downturn in the late 1970s and early 1980s also contributed to corporate welfare, since many cities and states now use public subsidies to attract jobs.

Corporate welfare is dangerous because it often substitutes government handouts instead of government regulation. When the federal government pays corporations to develop alternative fuel cars instead of requiring them to meet certain standards (a highly successful strategy that improved fuel economy and safety despite all the complaints from car manufacturers), the corporations happily pocket the cash and do as little as possible.

Corporate Welfare and "Free Trade"

Most progressives strongly oppose the antifree trade provisions imposed by corporate America, such as the tariffs designed to protect the sugar industry or the massive subsidies given to corporate farming, including tobacco farming. In 1999, U.S. government subsidies for farming exceeded $20 billion, amounting to nearly half of farm income and going far beyond the subsidies provided by any other country in the world, all of which American officials attack for infringing on free trade with excessive agricultural subsidies. These massive subsidies (most of which benefit large corporate farms rather than the traditional family farmer) came after Republicans promised to get rid of wasteful agricultural handouts in the 1996 Freedom to Farm Act. In 2000, the farming subsidies exceeded $23 billion (including $7.1 billion in "emergency aid" added by a conference committee without any public discussion in Congress), with 60 percent of the money paid to only 10 percent of farms.

The Reagan administration's attack on social programs and its "federalist" emphasis on turning power over to states and localities was a huge boon for corporate welfare. Urban renewal programs moved away from public improvements under federal guidance and toward direct bribes from cities and states to influential companies and developers. Instead of the federal government's determining which projects needed financing (a system vulnerable to political influence but generally successful), urban renewal at the end of the century had become a bidding war between states and cities. Using tax abatements and bonds, states and localities fight to offer the biggest bribes to companies. The public does not benefit from moving companies around from place to place and making public improvements designed to help these companies; only the corporations benefit from these welfare programs. Moreover, only those big businesses that have the resources to relocate and the political muscle to demand the bribes are the beneficiaries of this public largesse.

The corporate welfare queens also have been forced to respond to the growing influence of progressive movements to enforce environmental or health and safety regulations. The corporate welfare of the past was concealed by an ineffectual government that allowed companies to pollute the environment and harm its workers. Today, environmentally irresponsible policies require active lobbying to be continued, but the price is small compared with the welfare benefits available.

At times, corporate welfare is not just wasteful but dangerous. In the 1990s, the United States spent more than $10 billion covering bad loans to foreign countries for weapons purchases. Bad military loans for $2 billion went to Iraq, putting American weapons companies in the interesting position of profiting from both sides of the Persian Gulf War (while the American taxpayers paid to arm each side). Spending billions to subsidize the people shooting at American soldiers in order to help a few defense contractors increase their profits is probably the craziest example of corporate welfare and, considering the human and dollar cost of war, may be the single most wasteful case of corporate welfare.

Tax breaks are also a common form of corporate welfare. When the people who invest in companies pay a lower tax rate (the capital gains rate) than do people who work for a living, the main beneficiaries are the richest Americans and the corporations into which they invest their money into. Rich people pay half the maximum tax rate if they make their money from capital gains (20 percent) rather than work (39 percent). The 1997 cuts in the capital gains tax rate (from 28 percent to 20 percent) will cost taxpayers more than $21 billion over ten years, according to the Congressional Budget Office. This benefits the wealthiest Americans and the corporations in which they invest. But the biggest "tax expenditures" go directly to corporations with the influence to buy them.

The huge profits of big corporations have led many of them to use tax shelters and other schemes to avoid paying taxes. The Treasury Department revealed in 2000 that big corporations (with more than $1 billion in assets) in the 1990s have reported far less income to the IRS than to their shareholders. In 1992, the income reported to each was about equal, but by 1996 (the most recent data available) big corporations reported $420 billion in earnings to shareholders and only $301 billion to the IRS. If the rate of growth has continued, in 2000 more than $200 billion in earnings (or about one-third of corporate profits) could be concealed from the IRS. As a result of this corporate welfare by tax avoidance, individual taxpayers have to pay a bigger share.

If the tax evasion by "small" corporations (with less than $1 billion in assets) is added in, untold billions are being lost every year. According to Treasury Secretary Lawrence Summers, corporate tax shelters are the "most serious compliance issue facing the American tax system today." One reason is that Congress, legislating under the influence of money, frequently helps create tax breaks for big businesses. An obscure 1997 law changed the depreciation rules of the alternative minimum tax, which the *Congressional Quarterly* estimated will cost the U.S. Treasury $18.3 billion over ten years. That's one reason that in 1999, tax revenue from corporations declined 2 percent despite rising profits—a lower tax burden than at the beginning of the 1990s. From 1992 to 1999, the proportion of corporate taxes compared with individual income taxes paid fell more than 10 percent, a gap of nearly $70 billion.

Although corporations are supposed to pay 35 percent of their profits in taxes, corporate welfare tax breaks enable them to evade these taxes. A study by the Institute on Taxation and Economic Policy found that the effective tax rate paid by big corporations declined from 26.5 percent in 1988 to 20.1 percent in 1998. The discount from the actual 35 percent tax rate costs taxpayers $100 billion a year for the 250 largest corporations alone. The cost of these tax breaks is growing. At Cisco Systems, for example, the deferred federal tax benefit increased from $76 million in 1998 to $782 million in 2000.

A special exemption from the laws covering everyone else is another form of corporate welfare. The GAF Corporation and its $800 million owner Samuel Heyman launched a full-scale attack on asbestos litigation by pushing the "Fairness in Asbestos Compensation Act," which would limit the liability of asbestos companies such as GAF even in cases in which certain kinds of lung cancer have been proved to be caused by asbestos. The GAF's PAC and its family owners have spent $360,220 since 1995 in hard and soft money on Congress, not to mention huge lobbying expenses ($3.2 million in the last half of 1999 alone) and the creation of an industry front group (Coalition on Asbestos Resolution), to push their legislation. All together, since 1997 the asbestos industry has spent more than $15.2 million lobbying Congress in an effort to stop litigation against the deadly effects of its products.

Other industries have prospered from these special corporate welfare protections. In 1999, when Congress passed the District of Columbia Appropriations Act, Majority Leader Senator Trent Lott (D-Miss.) included a provision for "Superfund Recycling Equity," which relieved scrap metal dealers (who had given a rather paltry $300,000 to members of Congress in the 1990s) from any Superfund liability for toxic waste sites.

Unfortunately, many progressives pay little more than passing attention to corporate welfare. Much of the research on corporate welfare is done by the better-financed libertarian think tanks. As a result, the media and the policy wonks have only a limited picture of corporate welfare.

The key for progressives is showing that deregulation is also a form of corporate welfare. When companies impose social harms in order to make a buck, when they pollute air and water in pursuit of their profits, this is corporate welfare. Clean air is a natural resource, and when corporations freely pollute the air we breathe, it's as much of a gift to them as a tax break or a handout. Health and safety regulations are also part of what workers and consumers are entitled to, and when the public has to pay for injuries caused by irresponsible corporations, it's corporate welfare.

Although conservatives frequently rail against trial lawyers and urge tort reforms to protect corporations, the reality is that our overused legal system is produced by corporate influence on government. Many of the lawsuits for harms caused by corporations could be prevented by improving the government's regulation of dangerous practices. It's only in the "free market" state that problems are resolved by the expensive and often unequal system of litigation rather than by sound regulation.

There is no way to win a "government is good" argument in America; progressives can win arguments only by endorsing effective programs and denouncing wasteful spending.

Each year, a coalition of environmental and taxpayer groups puts together a report called "Green Scissors" to point out the wasteful government programs and subsidies that harm the environment. The "Green Scissors 2000" report found that nearly $50 billion in federal money is "used to pollute our nation's rivers, destroy habitats, create radioactive waste, and squander our natural resources"—and then taxpayer dollars often have to pay for the environmental cleanup.

One of the worst corporate welfare laws is also among the oldest: the 1872 Mining Law, which has allowed mining companies to take $245 billion in precious minerals from public lands without paying any royalties to the government. Mining companies can also buy public land with valuable minerals for $2.50 to $5 an acre. Worst of all, the government will pay to clean up half a million abandoned mine sites (including more than seventy Superfund sites), a cost of $32 billion to $72 billion to taxpayers.

The federal government also pays logging companies to destroy National Forests, causing soil erosion and habitat destruction. According to the General Accounting Office, the Forest Service lost more than $2 billion on its timber sales program from 1992 to 1997. By virtually giving away valuable trees and building expensive roads exclusively for logging, the federal government subsidizes this damage to our environment. While the public debates over the environment frequently pit the spotted owl versus logging workers, the true issue is the massive corporate welfare given to logging companies for environmentally wasteful practices

Huge amounts of government money regularly go to support corporate research and industry propaganda. In 1993, the National Shooting Sports Foundation, the gun industry's trade association, received $230,000 from the U.S. Fish and Wildlife Service to help teach children how to kill wildlife with guns. The foundation's trade publication, *S.H.O.T. Business*, advised: "There's a way to help ensure that new faces and pocketbooks will continue to patronize your business. Use the schools." Through a U.S. Department of Energy program, "Cooperative Research and Development Agreements," the Sandia National Laboratories did $300,000 in taxpayer-funded research in 1995 to help Disney World improve its nightly fireworks show.

Corporate welfare also includes "warfare welfare." The United States spends $7.6 billion a year in grants, subsidized financing, and tax breaks for companies that make and export armaments. The long-term cost of "warfare welfare" is far greater than this, though, since it must be measured in the human lives lost when these weapons are used. Defense industries are among the biggest tax evaders in the country: the top ten defense contractors made more than $21 billion in profits in 1998 but paid only $2.5 billion in taxes—less than 12 percent of their profits, one-third of the 35 percent tax rate, and the lowest of any industry in America.

Nearly everyone eats lunch, but not everybody pays for it equally. A construction worker who eats lunch with his buddies can't make his company pay for it and have the IRS reduce the corporation's taxes. However, when a business executive does exactly that, the worker actually ends up subsidizing the martini lunch for the CEO who gets paid 450 times as much. And when that construction worker goes to the baseball game that night, he sits in the stands and pays for his ticket and his beer and never expects the government to subsidize his entertainment. But when the CEO goes to the ballgame, he sits in the skybox and sips wine while the corporation picks up the bill, with some help from the taxpayers. It costs the government $5.5 billion a year to pay for the tax advantages from these lunches and entertainment expenses.

The advocates of corporate welfare try to appeal to progressives by claiming that these subsidies to corporations are necessary because they create jobs. After all, giving tax breaks for lunches and ball games helps employ waitresses and left-handed pitchers who might not otherwise get a chance at that work. Progressives can't be fooled by the rhetoric of jobs. All money creates jobs. If the government builds missiles, the missile makers employ people. If the government builds houses, the construction workers get jobs. If the government gives the money to poor people, the poor people buy groceries and clothing, and so there are jobs in the supermarkets and department stores. If the government returns the money to people by cutting taxes, these individuals spend the money and help employ people or invest the money and help entrepreneurs create businesses that employ people.

The issue is not job creation, but the kinds of jobs that are created and the goals that are being pursued. Subsidizing tobacco farmers in order to help farmers when the government is simultaneously trying to discourage smoking in order to save lives makes no sense whatsoever.

With corporate welfare like this, it may be tempting to adopt a libertarian line and suggest the abolition of most government programs. Although social programs designed to help the poor rather than the rich are only a small part of the government budget, these programs are crucial to the people who need them. The goal ought to be to fix the flaws and end corporate welfare, not to throw the infant-care program out with the dirty subsidies for the rich.

Chapter 19

THE DEFENSE INDUSTRY

How to Protect America by Cutting the Military

The most significant event to benefit progressives in the past two decades was the self-demolition of the Soviet Union. The American right had its greatest enemy (aside from American leftists) suddenly taken away, while the left had an enormous weight lifted from its shoulders.

STAR WARS FOLLIES

Of all the wasteful defense projects in the past century, "Star Wars" (or the Strategic Defense Initiative, SDI) stands as one of the great boondoggles in human history. Originally pushed by President Reagan in 1983, this wasteful gift of $60 billion to defense contractors has utterly failed to create a viable missile defense, and yet Star Wars has managed to survive the end of the

---

cold war, the dissolution of the Soviet Union, and the removal of any serious threats to American dominance in the world.

Now the Star Wars proponents are pushing to put an SDI system into effect, a plan that the Congressional Budget Office estimates will cost another $60 billion to protect America from a long-range missile launched by a "rogue" nation (even though none of them has this capacity). Personally, if I had spent $60 billion buying a TV that didn't work and somebody told me to buy another $60 billion TV from the same dealer, I'd think he was crazy.

The truth is that "rogue" nations rarely live up to the name, for none of them actually wants to contemplate the certain retaliation that would result from openly attacking the United States with a nuclear weapon. If a rogue nation ever wanted to launch a nuclear weapon at America, a long-range missile would be the least likely weapon of choice. For the leaders of Iraq, Iran, or North Korea, launching a nuclear missile at the United States would be an act of political (and probably literal) suicide. Instead of revealing exactly who launched the attack and using an unreliable long-range missile, a "rogue" nation would be far more likely to smuggle a nuclear weapon into the United States and detonate it without a trace left of the attacker. If tons of cocaine and thousands of illegal immigrants can pass through the border every year, why not a nuclear weapon?

If a "rogue nation" has a nuclear weapon, would it put it in an intercontinental ballistic missile or a box? The box is considerably cheaper, more anonymous, and less likely to fail. It's remarkably easy to put the box on a ship to New York Harbor, and by the time anyone stopped the boat to search it, the effect of a detonation would be devastating.

The only protection against nuclear weapons is denuclearization. Ending nuclear proliferation and eliminating nuclear weapons is the only feasible defense. If we're going to spend $60 billion, it should be toward that goal—except, of course, defense contractors and the recipients of their political donations wouldn't benefit from an antinuclear policy. And getting rid of nuclear weapons doesn't make all the technogeeks in the Pentagon go wobbly in the knees the way SDI does.

Even if a Star Wars defense worked for the United States, it would be little comfort to Europe and Israel if Iraq or Iran had a long-range nuclear missile capacity. Worse yet, SDI would violate the Ballistic Missile Defense Treaty, destabilize international relations, and may even cause the Russians to stop destroying its nuclear weapons.

After wasting hundreds of billions of dollars on sci-fi fantasies, the idea of throwing $60 billion more down the black hole called Star Wars should be unthinkable. Unfortunately, this last remnant of the cold war has blocked rational budget making, even if it can't stop real missiles.

The death of the Soviet Union also presents an opportunity, not yet taken, to use the resources devoted to military domination to lower taxes on the poor and improve our schools and social services. The military buildup of the 1980s, it's quite clear now, was never necessary: only an enormous miscalculation of Soviet military and economic power could have caused such a vast waste of money. In the history of the world, no nation has ever exercised the kind of total military domination that the United States now has. Nonetheless, both the Democrats and the Republicans have pushed for large increases in the military budget beyond the $300 billion mark. The peace dividend, it turns out, is being used to buy more weapons.

There is no need for a military budget that far exceeds any other country in the world. With $800 billion spent worldwide on the military each year, America's $300 billion military outlays are more than the next seven to twelve (depending on estimates) largest military forces combined.

The United States military has no competitors on the planet. Peacekeeping operations in Bosnia, for example, require very few troops and only a tiny proportion of the military budget. Even the massive bombing of Iraq, which killed tens of thousands of troops and innocent civilians, represented only a small part of America's military power and annual budget.

PROGRESSIVES AND THE GOOD WAR:
WHY MILITARY INTERVENTION IS WRONG

The most common excuse used by liberals to justify a large defense budget is the need for foreign intervention in noble causes. Progressives have usually been skeptical of the idea that wars can be fought and thousands killed in a glorious war. But even the left has been split over conflicts such as Kosovo, where many progressives believed that military action was necessary to prevent genocide.

Progressives shouldn't rush to adopt the "good war" and the destruction it justifies. Bombing is one of the least effective military policies, since it is difficult to control the reaction to violence. In Kosovo, the mass migration that followed the U.S. bombings could just have easily taken the form of mass killings, which the U.S. military would have been ill prepared to stop. A successful military action must not harm the civilian population of a country. In Iraq, the U.S. sanctions stopping food and medicine from entering the borders have killed thousands of children every year, but Saddam Hussein's position has actually been strengthened by this irrational policy.

Progressives are globalists, and it is essential for the United States to assist the rest of world in preventing genocide and war whenever possible. Instead of killing people in order to make peace, the best approach is for the United States to function as a peacekeeping operation within the United Nations. UN intervention to prevent war and slaughter is a legitimate and necessary

(continued)

action, and peacekeeping operations typically have very low casualty rates on all sides and are far less expensive than a hot war. The United States should work within the UN because it helps build international support for the actions. In reality, the United States must do so because so many past interventions by Americans have been designed to prop up failing dictatorships rather than to protect human lives and human rights. The United States has far less credibility on the international scene than the UN, so it is necessary to rely on an international force on those rare occasions when intervention is needed.

The enormous peacetime military budget is the largest single source of corporate welfare, but until the 1980s it was relatively small. The massive increases during the Reagan administration, however, gave defense contractors considerable profits to invest in lobbying activities.

The Defense Department is the most wasteful part of our government, and yet no one proposes ending the military as we know it. The stories about a $640 toilet seat and a $437 tape measure are infamous. Less well known is the fact that between 1985 and 1995, the Defense Department "lost" $13 billion handed out to weapons contractors, and another $15 billion could not be accounted for. Now the Pentagon has spent millions to subsidize corporate mergers of defense contractors. It's probably the only example of a customer eagerly paying to reduce the competition available.

The military dominance of the United States over the rest of the world is unparalleled in human history. No great empire—not Egypt, not Rome, not anyone—has ever before had such complete power over the entirety of the Earth. Most of the nations of the world would have difficulty killing even a single American soldier during a devastating U.S. attack.

In the past, the military budget was justified by the need to stay above the Soviet Union's military spending. With that Communist empire lying in ruins and its defense forces almost eviscerated, what possible reason could there be to continue running up cold war defense budgets? At the time of its war with the United States, Iraq had one of the most powerful military forces in the Third World, and it suffered one of the most lopsided losses in history.

Even during the cold war, the military budget was inflated far beyond reasonable needs. Future historians will certainly look back at America in the 1980s and 1990s and marvel that a country could waste so much money buying billion-dollar toys for its generals to play with.

Today, the military-industrial-political complex scrambles to invent new excuses for the bloated defense budget. With imaginary scenarios of fighting two major wars simultaneously (something the United States has never done before and almost certainly would not need to do), hawks try to justify growing the defense budget far beyond its needs.

There is no military need for the current size of the Defense Department. Our permanent, large standing army spread around the world is an anomaly leftover from the cold war— never before has the United States maintained such a huge force during peacetime. Now that the cold war is over, it's time to return to a more reasonable military force. By eliminating many foreign military bases that could be staffed by our allies (our economic competitors in Japan and Germany currently are subsidized by American defense spending) and by slowly reducing our standing army, the United States can be adequately protected by its current high-tech weapons and by a large force of reserves that, as in the Gulf War, can easily be called up for active duty. Reserve forces are much cheaper than a standing army and also allow our soldiers to contribute to the economy.

Ultimately, the military strength of the United States for the next century will not depend on how many expensive explosive toys it has at the moment or the size of its standing army. Rather, U.S. security will depend on its economic growth and the education of its citizens. Future wars will be more computerized than ever, and a poorly educated standing army will be far less important than a well-educated citizenry. Today, wars are essentially fought with money, and diverting some current military funding to pay off the debt will do far more to increase our future military potential than spending it today on weapons that will quickly be outdated.

Much of the United States' military budget and foreign aid is used to subsidize defense contractors with plants in influential districts and to buy weapons that are ultimately used to kill innocents and even American soldiers. The United States exports 60 percent of the weapons sold worldwide, weaponry that is then used to justify even more defense spending. A secret FBI report revealed that it was a U.S. AN-M41 fragmentation bomb that exploded in Santo Domingo, Colombia on December 13, 1998, killing at least nineteen civilians, including several small children (the Colombian military had blamed the bombing on leftists). The bomb was part of the billions of dollars worth of weaponry given by the United States to military dictatorships around the world. News of how American weapons were being used to murder innocents did not stop Congress and the Clinton administration from giving $1.3 billion in military aid to Colombia in the name of stopping the drug trade. The massive military-industrial complex promotes war around the world, not peace.

Progressives don't need to argue for dismantling the military. To the contrary, the left ought to propose a military budget that will make the United States by far the most powerful military force in the world. But thanks to all the waste in the Defense Department and the end of the cold war, the United States could dominate the world while spending about half of what it currently does. Progressives don't need to urge extensive cuts that might make the United States a second-rate military force: a gradual reduction of the military budget to $150 billion to $200 billion a year would still make America the dominant power in the world and easily capable of all necessary military action. All that extra money (about $1 trillion per decade) could be used for debt reduction and investment in education to increase the long-term military security of the United States.

WHY WE NEED THE UNITED NATIONS

Progressives must be globalists: we believe in having international organizations that can work to promote fairness between nations and international efforts at justice, from international law courts to attempts to narrow the gap between rich and poor nations.

Unfortunately, progressives in America must fight an uphill battle against Jesse Helms and an army of paranoids with vibrant imaginations. There are no black UN helicopters surveilling the United States, waiting to take over the country. There is no conspiracy to destroy U.S. sovereignty and freedom. In truth, the United States runs the UN like a puppet master, except that puppet masters usually pay for their puppets and the United States owes a huge sum of money. Because of our veto in the Security Council and our power around the world, the UN does virtually nothing without U.S. endorsement.

Progressives have legitimate critiques of international organizations such as the World Bank, the International Monetary Fund, and the UN, all of which are too beholden to U.S. corporations, too devoted to large development projects and banking bailouts rather than genuine economic improvements, and far too indifferent to the needs of the poor.

(continued)

But if we did not have a UN, we would have to invent it. The UN enables the international community to act against petty dictators and to make positive efforts to improve the conditions faced by the poor around the world. Of course, the UN must represent more than just a military force; it must prevent wars by fighting against poverty and resolving national conflicts. When an international police force is needed, the UN—not the United States—must serve in this role.

Chapter 20

SAVING SOCIAL SECURITY

It's common to hear those fearful about the future fiscal stability of Social Security cite a poll claiming that more young adults believe in the existence of aliens on Earth than believe that they will receive Social Security benefits.

I believe it, too.

Well, not the nonsense about aliens, although Steve Forbes has shaken my firm belief that we are alone on Earth. But I do believe—or perhaps *hope* is the term—that I will never receive a penny from Social Security. That's because I hope to be very rich when I grow old, and I also hope Social Security will be means tested, so that someone who's appallingly wealthy (namely, the future me) won't receive a government check.

Of course, that's not why so many young adults imagine that Social Security won't be a part of their retirement. They believe a lot of nonsense about the Social Security "crisis," a crisis that is no more real than the tabloid stories about extraterrestrials probing and impregnating Earthlings.

The Social Security "crisis" is created by making lowball estimates of the growth of the American economy. The crisis predictors imagine that GDP growth in the future will be below 1.5 percent. But if GDP growth averages only 2.07 percent—far below its productivity in the past decade—Social Security will be financially secure for the next seventy-five years. Considering that GDP grew 2.2 percent during the weak 1979–1995 period, it's impossible to believe that 1.5 percent GDP growth is likely in the twenty-first century, and if the economy does turn out to be this weak, the stock market will fail to continue its massive increases, so a "privatization" scheme wouldn't help anyone.

Nor are today's workers going to be left penniless if for some reason the economy grows slower than 2 percent per year. The only result of a Social Security shortfall would be marginally lower benefits for retirees. There would be no problem at all in meeting the future obligations of Social Security unless conservatives "privatize" Social Security by allowing young workers to partially opt out of the system.

Even if there were a crisis in Social Security, an easy solution would be to eliminate the ceiling on payroll taxes. Currently, the wealthy don't have to pay any payroll taxes on income above $80,000. As a result, poor and middle-income workers actually pay a larger proportion of their income in payroll taxes than the rich do, even though the wealthy end up with biggest Social Security paychecks when they retire. A worker who earns $50,000 pays the 6.2 percent payroll tax, which is matched by her employer. A CEO making $15 million, by contrast, only pays 0.03 percent of his income for payroll taxes. The regular worker in this case pays 200 times as much of her income in payroll taxes as the CEO does.

The payroll tax also subsidizes employment of the rich because of the company's contribution to Social Security. Because of the low cap on Social Security, companies—like their employees—pay much more for low-wage and middle-income workers, whereas millionaire CEOs are virtually untaxed.

Social Security is not a perfect progressive system, even if it is an improvement on the free market without a safety net. The biggest problem with Social Security is the regressive payroll tax that for many of the working poor represents the largest tax they pay. A progressive program for Social Security ought to lift the cap on payroll taxes for the wealthy (but put a cap on payouts when they retire) and use the money to sharply reduce the payroll taxes on the poor (while still giving them credit in the Social Security system). Lower-income workers would have a bigger paycheck while still keeping the Social Security system financially secure.

The fears about Social Security are being promoted by a lot of people who want to see Social Security "privatized"—that is, cutting a big hole in the social safety net and hoping that the stock market will rise high enough for everyone to buy a trampoline to put in its place. It's not only risky to tie so much of our economic health to the stock market, but it could create the very crisis in Social Security that is feared.

Social Security works as a pay-as-you-go government program: today's workers provide the money to support current retirees. A thirty-year-old worker who pays 2 percent of her income (about 15 percent of the payroll tax revenue for that worker) in Social Security taxes may end up slightly better off when she retires. But for the next forty years, the Social Security system will be deprived of that 15 percent of its income. For a system supposedly in crisis (and in reality at a breakeven point), losing 15 percent of the money from current payees makes future cuts in Social Security virtually inevitable. The result will be a fiscal crisis in Social Security when this money isn't immediately available to pay current retirees who haven't had the opportunity to privatize their Social Security.

The only way to "privatize" Social Security without wrecking it is to raise payroll taxes for twenty or thirty years and use the added revenue for personal savings accounts. Many of the plans to privatize Social Security are nothing more than a tax increase to compel investment. The conservative Cato Institute has attacked Republican congressmen Bill Archer (R-Tex.) and Clay Shaw (R-Fl.) for proposing a Social Security "reform" of this kind that would increase payroll taxes by $2.6 trillion more than the current system through 2034. But since workers can already use 401(k) plans and IRAs to save privately for their retirement, no one is demanding to privatize Social Security except those who want to destroy the program. At least the conservatives who plan to raise taxes in order to privatize Social Security are honest about its costs; the ones who must cut Social Security benefits to afford "privatization" are lying to the public by refusing to confront this economic inevitability.

Another phony plan to "privatize" Social Security is to invest the funds from the Social Security trust fund in the stock market, which will mostly enhance the money taken by brokers. The wisdom of investing government funds in a volatile stock market is debatable, especially because there is no Social Security trust fund. It's an accounting fiction. In reality, the money from Social Security surpluses is used to counter deficit spending or maintain a surplus for loans to cover the national debt. All government money goes into the same pool: if Social Security funds aren't used to pay off the debt, then the government must increase its borrowing.

In essence, the plan to invest Social Security money in the stock market is the equivalent of somebody's borrowing money for stock speculation and hoping she'll make more money playing the stock market than she'll lose paying interest on the loan. There's a reason that banks are reluctant to loan money for stock speculation: the stock market is too risky to be certain of large profits from it. Although a stock market crash right now would be a disaster for the American economy, and if substantial amounts of government money were lost with it, the Social Security system could easily collapse. Stock investments are an excellent way to use surplus funds; but no stock adviser recommends that anyone in debt (such as America is) borrow more money and hope that the stock market will provide a big payoff.

Rather than "saving" Social Security from this phony crisis, the political establishment in Washington is giving away more money to the wealthy, apparently hoping to weaken Social Security. In 2000, Congress passed a law to pay out more Social Security benefits to the 6 percent of wealthy senior citizens who are still earning a high salary. This was justified as removing some of the "penalty" on people who continue to work. But is Social Security a retirement program or a subsidy for the wealthy? People who love their work still can make more money working than retiring. Why give away so much money to the richest elderly people who do not need it to survive? There are good reasons to allow poor senior citizens to work without penalty, especially if their Social Security benefits are below the poverty line. But it seems very odd to pass large tax breaks for the rich on Social Security at a time when hordes of Chicken Littles are shouting about the financial sky falling.

Robert Kuttner of the liberal *American Prospect* argues that unless the elderly working rich are paid high benefits, "the broad popular support for Social Security would simply evaporate." Progressives should challenge the belief that one must pay off the well-off in order to help the poor.

The public is far more concerned about the financial future of Social Security than about the prospect of redistribution.

Changing the rules to give money away to the working elderly who are rich will drain Social Security's funding even more, and the sole fiscal benefit of this decision (potentially higher tax revenues from having a few more senior citizens working) will probably be returned to the wealthy in a tax break.

Trickle-Down Welfare

Too many progressives fundamentally distrust democracy. They believe the American public is too self-interested to actually help the poor. Hence, the need not only to have universal programs but also to allow the distribution to be distorted so that the well-off benefit more than the poor.

The problem is not that we provide Social Security and public schools and public parks to the wealthy but that the rich almost always get a greater share of public resources than the poor do. Go to almost any wealthy area in America, and you'll find well-financed public schools, nice public parks, and retirees making a livable wage from Social Security. Go to almost any poor area in America, and you're likely to find underfinanced, inadequate schools, neglected public parks, and retirees struggling to get by on far less money from the government than their wealthy counterparts.

America spends much more money on building and maintaining roads for the commuting needs of well-off suburbanites than on providing adequate public transit for the working poor. We spend far more money on public schools for the average rich kid than for the average poor kid, despite the greater need to help impoverished students. We spend more money on parks catering to the wealthy and neglect the public space in poorer neighborhoods. In a thousand different towns, you can see the disinvestment in public institutions for the poor. In most of America, the potholes in the streets, the cracks in the broken sidewalks, and the decrepit state of the public schools correlate almost perfectly with the poverty of the population.

Government benefits from universal programs do not simply "leak" to the rich; they pour out in a massive flood, leaving little left to help the poor. Imagine if the money spent building high-tech labs and Olympic-sized swimming pools for schools in wealthy areas with low tax rates could instead be devoted to buying up-to-date textbooks in poor schools.

Trickle-down theories were thoroughly discredited during the Reagan administration, when huge tax breaks for the rich and corporate subsidies never trickled down to the poor. Progressives have adopted a trickle-down philosophy about government programs. Big benefits for wealthy communities are deemed necessary because the poor will get a small piece of the pie. Like trickle-down economics, trickle-down government is failing the poor. Too much of the money is going to the wealthy, and the political constraints on enlarging the government make it impossible for the poor to catch up.

The unequal distribution of government resources is not only unjust, it's also inefficient. Many Americans work long hours trying to make enough money to afford a house in a wealthy neighborhood with nice parks and excellent schools. Imagine how much money we could save the country if we provided enough public investment in all our schools and parks to benefit everybody where they already live.

Perhaps it's time for progressives to change their tactics. Instead of making sure that every government program has a massive "leak" to the well-off in order to gain public support, we ought to try fixing some of these unfair leaks. If progressives demanded equal treatment of rich and poor in government-financed schools, roads, sidewalks, garbage, police, parks, pollution, health care, libraries, and Social Security, the response from the public would not be a complete abandonment of public institutions in favor of a libertarian fantasy. On the contrary, equality would probably increase public support for these services and a demand for more improvements.

If paying all Social Security recipients equally is too radical for anyone to contemplate, at the very least progressives can demand that all workers pay the same percentage of their income for Social Security taxes—instead of the current system, which offers a huge tax break to the rich by capping the payroll tax. With the massive influx of money gained from lifting the cap, we could greatly improve the financial health of Social Security and offer a cut in payroll tax rates to 90 percent of working Americans. Would that leave universal social insurance in shreds?

Progressives need to realize that the biggest barrier to reform of government institutions (such as the regressive payroll tax) does not come from the public but from our corrupt political institutions. The problem is that the wealthy have too much power in Washington (and the state capitals and localities around the country). The old adage that "power corrupts" perhaps should be updated to "power allocates money." The wealthiest Americans have enormous influence to block progressive reforms.

The case is not hopeless. Progressives can sometimes become so pragmatic that the most persuasive arguments about equality and fairness aren't even voiced. If the idea of equality for government benefits is pushed and gets a fair hearing, there's an opportunity to sway public opinion without sacrificing our beliefs to the mundane world of politics run by the wealthy.

Chapter 21

THE FUTURE OF PROGRESSIVES

Generation Left

If progressives are going to rise to power in the twenty-first century, they will need to convince a new generation that the ideas of the left can transform American politics.

The youth of America already are cynical and skeptical of the current system. They're ready for change. Unfortunately, they're also skeptical of the possibility of political transformation, and they associate progressive ideas with the failures of liberalism.

Call us Generation Left. This, like most slogans, is a complete misnomer. Generation Left is not a monolithic generation, nor are younger people noticeably more progressive than the baby boomers of the 1960s who preceded them or the senior citizens who remember when the labor movement actually mattered for more than providing spare campaign cash to the Democrats.

Generation naming is always a dubious enterprise: the term Generation X began with Douglas Coupland's novel about guideless slackers, and since then Generation X (and its less popular follow-up, Generation Y) has mostly served as a marketing slogan. Coupland's phrase, though, was a perfect description of Generation Left: unsure of itself, with no clear identity, a giant unknown in generational terms. What's been missed, though, is the progressive potential of these young (and some now turning nearly middle aged) adults and of the generations that are coming after them.

The term *Generation Left* refers to a widespread shift in American values during the twentieth century, and most of the changes were enacted by our more courageous elders. The difference between Generation Left and the older generations is that the new generation grew up taking progressive goals for granted. Generation Left assumes that when corporations endanger our health or the environment, the government will step in to stop them.

Generation Left is also a generation opposed to bigotry. Needless to say, racism, sexism, and homophobia still persist, often in horrific forms. But this is the first American generation to which these ideas are generally considered shameful. Generation Left grew up learning that racist jokes weren't acceptable and that homosexuality could be. Generation Left grew up in an America where formal discrimination was banned, where the horror of illegal abortions did not exist, and where the notion of equality—if rarely the reality—was held to be the ideal.

When the baby boomers grew up, Martin Luther King Jr. was a dangerous radical followed by the FBI and demonized by the mainstream; when Generation Left grew up, King had become a martyr honored by a federal holiday. In the process, much of King's radicalism has been forgotten, but the mere fact that a

1960s leftist can now be honored by the entire country shows how far progressive ideas have come.

It's common to assume that Generation Left holds conservative views. After all, Generation Left grew up with Ronald Reagan and Ollie North and George Bush on their TV screens, with "greed is good" as their guiding ideology, with Walter Mondale and Michael Dukakis as their models of failed liberalism.

Many members of Generation Left have never seriously considered progressive ideas. Unlike the seniors who struggled to establish labor unions and the New Deal or the baby boomers who brought us the protests of the 1960s, this generation was raised on bad sit-coms and never saw progressive politics in action. Their American history classes never got past World War II; their college campuses were full of well-financed conservative groups and newspapers; and the term *liberal* was an insult. Generation Left is also a generation subject to corporate influences, wearing our Nike shoes and our logo T-shirts and watching more commercials than any generation in history.

The leftism of this generation is only an unrealized potential, and it might never come to fruition. Generation Left is not a progressive generation simply awaiting a leader or an organization. It will take hard work to convince Generation Left to care about politics and to support progressive values.

This won't happen merely by making earnest pleas for people to cast away their cynicism and vote for the lesser of two evils. Cynicism is not a disease on our political system; it's the canary dying in the coal mine, the warning signal that tells us when the oxygen of freedom and democracy is running out. The danger is not that we will have more cynics warning us of the dangers we are headed into; the danger is that the cynics will start dying of ideological asphyxiation, becoming limp, apathetic, apolitical, and indifferent. With each dead cynic is born a lost citizen who no longer believes in politics.

Generation Left needs a different kind of progressive movement. Generation Left has little interest in labor unions, for few of us will ever belong to one, and fewer still will promote one. Generation Left has little interest in political parties. The old political machines are dead, and party politics is the adult refuge for all those losers we elected to student government so they could pad their résumés.

Generation Left will not be found marching en masse in Washington, D.C. or hanging out at the protest against the injustice of the day. This generation votes less often than any other in American history; its members are cynical and disillusioned with conventional politics. Generation Left will not become an openly progressive force unless the left convinces this generation that it offers something different from the status quo.

Appealing to the young doesn't mean pandering to their interests (free MTV for all!) or engaging in generational warfare. Instead, Generation Left is the strongest embodiment of a movement among all Americans, regardless of age, race, gender, or class: the disillusionment with a corrupt political system and the desire to find an alternative.

Progressives can offer a genuine alternative to the status quo with policies that help the majority of Americans. Progressives can help end the dominance of the special corporate interests that currently are in power, regardless of which party wins.

An America run according to progressive values won't be easy to achieve. The enemies of equality are well financed and well established in power. Progressives need to communicate the message that their ideas are the embodiment of American ideals of equality and justice. By showing that progressive beliefs represent the majority and by appealing to the power of democracy, progressives can continue to change American politics.

ABOUT THE AUTHOR

John K. Wilson is the author of *The Myth of Political Correctness: The Conservative Attack on Higher Education* and *Newt Gingrich: Capitol Crimes and Misdemeanors*.